PRAYER THE FOUNDATION FOR JUSTICE

Dr. Kimberly K. Clayton

Prayer the Foundation for Justice

Copyright © 2023, 2024 by Dr. Kimberly K. Clayton

All rights reserved. No part of this publication may be reproduced, stored in a retrieval system, or transmitted in any form by any means, electronic, mechanical, photocopying, recording, or otherwise, without the prior permission of the author.

Without in any way limiting the author's exclusive rights under copyright, any use of this publication to "train" generative artificial intelligence (AI) technologies to generate text or any other format is **expressly prohibited**. The author reserves all rights to license uses of this work for generative AI training and development of machine learning language models.

Self-Published IngramSpark by Dr. Kimberly K. Clayton 2024

itsprayingtime2020@gmail.com

ISBN: 979-8-218-40268-6 (paperback)

Library of Congress Control Number: 2024907419

Front & Back Cover designed by Dr. Kimberly K. Clayton

Photos retrieved from iStockphoto.com:
Front Cover: Praying Woman Silhouette by grace21, Stock Photo ID: 476359222
Upload date June 6, 2015

Back Cover: Protest Photo by Drazen Zigic, Stock Photo ID: 1249019653
Upload date June 26, 2020

Scriptures were retrieved through Biblegateway.com

Photo(s) of Dr. Kimberly K. Clayton were taken by Photographer Samantha of PicturePeople 2021, 2022 with Photography Permission Releases

Acknowledgments

I would like to thank Father God, Jesus Christ and the Holy Spirit for all their help and inspiration with this thesis research paper. Thank you for hearing and answering my prayers.

To my late Mom, Mrs. Jones, who showed me how to pray and to be faithful to prayer intercession. To my dad, Mr. Jones, my daughter, Elise and my "bonus children" thank you for loving me and being there when I needed each of you most.

I would like to thank Dr. Elaine O. Spencer for her loving, supporting, and winning attitude that has encouraged me not to give up on my thesis paper, but to finish for the glory of God.

To my friend who started her thesis and couldn't finish; I'm finishing in honor of your late memory and what you meant to me.

To every mail carrier that delivered my books no matter, how hot or cold it was outside, THANK YOU! You are appreciated.

Thank you to everyone who took time to sincerely pray for me.

This is just the beginning, and I am happy to have come this far by faith. I am looking forward to doing more research on prayer and even more with The Prayer Empowerment Theory!

Abstract

Prayer is the foundation to justice. Biblical leaders who had the common thread of prayer, the majority of the time did not venture out without praying first. Even our modern-day leaders who face great odds consistently state they pray every day and throughout the day. Great leaders understand that even though they are called to do a task, they know they can't do the task in their own strength. Fighting for justice cannot be done without prayer because history shows us that the opposition is relentless.

Therefore, prayer is the tool, the KEY that gives individuals access to the source (Father God) who gives them strength. God strengthens (empowers) our leaders to keep advocating for justice on behalf of those who need it most. The opposition often denies that any injustices have occurred! There are adversaries who are willing to torment leaders in their fight for justice. Some leaders are even required to pay the ultimate price with their own life. A great leader cannot take on the tasks, death threats, harassment, and hatred without a solid prayer life. The fight for justice starts with prayer, continues with prayer, ends with prayer, combined with effort and empowered action by leaders who never gave up!

I present that prayer is the foundation to justice through the lens of The Prayer Empowerment Theory: I researched, studied, and analyzed the prayer lives of Ruby Bridges, Mother Teresa, Coretta Scott King, Martin Luther King Jr., Nelson Mandela, and Desmond Tutu. The study was conducted through content and questionnaire analysis of autobiographies, biographies, documented interviews, articles, movies, museum exhibits, etc. Please note that **Jesus Christ's prayer life was studied throughout this thesis research paper, and He was the KEY ROLE MODEL for the six "Great Names".**

CONTENTS

CHAPTER 1 - INTRODUCTION 1
    THESIS OBJECTIVES & SCOPE 1
    DEFINING PRAYER & IT'S RELEVANCE 2
    DEFINING JUSTICE & IT'S SIGNIFICANCE 11
    JUSTICE VS INJUSTICE CHART 12
    WHY I RESEARCHED PRAYER & JUSTICE? 16

CHAPTER 2 – THE PRAYER & JUSTICE CONNECTION 23
    INTRODUCTION 23
    SCOPE & RESEARCH GAP 24
    ARGUMENTS FOR THE PRAYER & JUSTICE CONNECTION 25
    ARGUMENTS AGAINST THE PRAYER & JUSTICE CONNECTION 42
    CONCLUSION 47

CHAPTER 3 – THE PRAYER EMPOWERMENT THEORY 50
    THE PRAYER EMPOWERMENT THEORY 50
    RESEARCH STEPS 51
    CONTENT ANALYSIS METHODOLOGY 52
    THE PRAYER EMPOWERMENT THEORY CONCEPT MAPS 53
    THE SIX GREAT NAMES PRAYERS & ACCOMPLISHMENTS VS AFFLICTIONS 56
    QUESTIONNAIRE TESTING METHODOLOGY 58
    THE PRAYER EMPOWERMENT THEORY FOUR CORE OUTLINES 59
    EVALUATION OF THE METHODOLOGIES 61

CHAPTER 4 – THE PRAYER LIVES OF SIX GREAT NAMES 65
    RUBY BRIDGES 65
    MOTHER TERESA 69
    CORETTA SCOTT KING 73
    MARTIN LUTHER KING JR. 81
    NELSON MANDELA (MANDIBA) 85
    DESMOND TUTU 91

CHAPTER 5 - CONCLUSION 99
    RESULTS 99
    SUMMARY 101
    CONCLUSION 105

APPENDIX A – THE PRAYER EMPOWERMENT QUESTIONNAIRE	**109**
APPENDIX B – THE PRAYER FOUNDATION QUESTIONNAIRE	**110**
APPENDIX C – THE FIGHT FOR JUSTICE QUESTIONNAIRE	**111**
APPENDIX D – THE PRAYER OUTCOME QUESTIONNAIRE	**112**
APPENDIX E – GLOSSARY	**113**
APPENDICES F – Q	**120**
The Prayer Empowerment Theory Concept Maps	120
APPENDIX R – THE SIX GREAT NAMES PRAYERS	**133**
APPENDIX S – ACCOMPLISHMENTS VS. AFFLICTIONS	**136**
BIBLIOGRAPHY	**141**
ABOUT THE AUTHOR	**149**
MY PRAYER FOR YOU	**150**

PRAYER THE FOUNDATION FOR JUSTICE

Chapter 1 - Introduction

Thesis Objectives & Scope

This thesis will show why the **Great Names of Justice/The Great Names/The Great** or Humanitarians are seen as being people who were extraordinary that will remain in history forever. (See Appendix E – Glossary) I will prove that prayer was the starting point, the **Foundation** that thrusted The Great into **Action** for justice, no matter how impossible the odds were against them. (See Appendix E – Glossary) I explored the prayer lives of six great names, Ruby Bridges, Mother Teresa, Coretta Scott King, Martin Luther King Jr., Nelson Mandela, and Desmond Tutu. The research will show that they did not do it in their own strength, they had help from Almighty God through their committed prayer life.

The scope of my thesis focuses on **Faith** in Jesus Christ, God Almighty, and the Holy Spirit, prayer, justice, injustice, Biblical scriptures, and insights from the Holy Bible as true and authentic as saying, "It's the Gospel of Jesus Christ." I will not cover whether God exists, various types of justice, revenge, or other faiths in this thesis. (See Appendix E – Glossary)

The **Prayer Empowerment Theory** is comprised of four Core Outlines: **Prayer Empowerment Theory, Prayer Foundation, Fight for Justice and Prayer Outcome.** (See Chapters 3 & 5, Appendices A-D) The Prayer Empowerment Theory terms are bolded, the definitions are listed in the Glossary in Appendix E.

Reviewing the terms makes it easier to understand how the Prayer Empowerment Theory works and applies to the six Great Names of Justice. Since the Prayer Empowerment Theory is a new theory, the Terms and Concept Maps are mentioned at least once in the Introduction Chapter. The terms, definitions and concepts of the Prayer Empowerment Theory will be found throughout the rest of this thesis, but especially in Chapter 4 The Prayer Lives of Six Great Names.

Defining Prayer & It's Relevance

Well, what is prayer? It's important to know **Prayer** is a conversation with GOD the Father, where one talks to God and listens to God (See Appendix E - Glossary). Father GOD is the one who created us and desires a close relationship with us. It is important to note that these aren't the only types of prayer, but there are different types of prayer: **Prayer of Adoration, Forgiveness, Intercession, Lamenting, Thanksgiving, Petitions/Request, Silent Christ Centered Prayer, Empowerment Prayer, Serenity Prayer, and Successor Prayer.** (See Appendices E – Glossary and R – Six Great Names Prayers). These forms of prayer are a very strong indication of a quality prayer life and close personal relationship with Jesus Christ. As the six great names prayed the more **Prayer Transformation** took place, where one grows through the stages of prayer until one is a divine collaborator/partner with God. Where one has learned, **"JUST DON'T ASK WHAT GOD CAN DO FOR YOU, ASK GOD WHAT YOU CAN DO FOR HIM."** (See Appendices E – Glossary and G – Prayer Transformation Map).

Father GOD and Jesus Christ, the Son of God paid the ultimate price to reconcile humanity back to Himself. There are scriptures that helps us to see why prayer and obedience are so important in the gift of salvation. Through Jesus Christ we must look at an important scripture that is one of my favorites Philippians 2:8, but for more understanding I will include Philippians 2:4-11 NIV:

4) Not looking to your own interests but each of you to the interests of the others. 5) In your relationships with one another, have the same mindset as Christ Jesus: 6) Who, being in very nature (of) God, did not consider equality with God something to be used to his own advantage; 7) rather he made himself nothing, by taking the very nature of a servant, being made in human likeness. 8) And being found in appearance as man, he humbled himself by becoming obedient to death – even death on a cross! 9) Therefore God exalted him to the highest place and gave him the name that is above every name, 10) that at the name of Jesus every knee should bow, in heaven and on earth and under the earth, 11) and every tongue acknowledge that Jesus Christ is Lord to the glory of God the Father.

Jesus Christ and the Great Names fully embody this level of **Obedience** defined as when one receives instructions from God Almighty one carries those instructions out with courage, determination, and humility. Because of their obedience they exemplified being **Doers of God's Word** faithfully throughout their lives here on earth. (See Appendices E – Glossary and M – Obedience Map).
And John 3:16-21 NIV really makes it clearer.

16) For God so loved the world that he gave his one and only Son, that whoever believes in him shall not perish but have eternal life. 17) For God did not send his Son into the world to condemn the world, but to save the world through him. 18) Whoever believes in him is not condemned, but whoever does not believe stands condemned already because they have not believed in the name of God's one and only Son. 19) This is the verdict: Light has come into the world, but people loved darkness instead of light because their deeds were evil. 20) Everyone who does evil hates the light, and

will not come into the light for fear that their deeds will be exposed. 21) But whoever lives by the truth comes into the light, so that it may be seen plainly that what they have done has been done in the sight of God. Let's look at a few more scriptures 2 Corinthians 5:18-21:

18) All this is from God, who reconciled us to himself through Christ and gave us the ministry of reconciliation: 19) that God was reconciling the world to himself in Christ, not counting men's sins against them. And he has committed to us the message of reconciliation. 20) We are therefore Christ's ambassadors, as though God were making his appeal through us. We implore you on Christ's behalf: Be reconciled to God. 21) God made him who had no sin to be sin for us, so that in him we might become the righteousness of God.

Romans 10:9-10 NIV:

9) If you declare with your mouth, "Jesus is Lord," and believe in your heart that God raised him from the dead, you will be saved. 10) For it is with your heart that you believe and are justified, and it is with your mouth that you profess your faith and are saved.

It's important that we understand that Father God loved us (humanity) so much that He gave up His only Son, so He did not have to live eternally without us, and we do not have to live eternally without Him. Since Jesus Christ reconciles us to the Father we have direct access to Father God, no longer do we have to go through the priest only. Salvation gives us so much more than just going to **Heaven**, it has given us the beauty of being in a loving, intimate and very real relationship with Father God through Jesus Christ. We must remember before Jesus Christ was crucified his **Disciples (Kingdom Believers)** asked Him to teach them how to pray. If prayer wasn't important, it wouldn't be in the Bible well over 500 times.

Luke 11:1-4 NIV:

1) One day Jesus was praying in a certain place. When he finished, one of his disciples said to him, "Lord, teach us to pray, just as John taught his disciples."

2) He said to them, "When you pray say: " ' Father, hallowed be your name, your kingdom come.

3) Give us each day our daily bread.

4) Forgive us our sins, for we also forgive everyone who sins against us. And lead us not into temptation."

Jesus Christ gave a model for prayer that **Acknowledges God** the Father with reverence – a Godly respect and honor; that Heaven would come to earth through God's divine will and through our obedience and servanthood (See Appendices E – Glossary and H – Acknowledges God Map). That we ask God to provide our daily needs like food and other necessities. That we confess our sins and ask God to forgive our sins (Romans 3:23), and that we too must forgive those who have sinned against us. Please note FORGIVENESS is not optional, IT'S REQUIRED. That God will lead us from temptation or the evil one or the ways of the evil one. Jesus knew that he would only be with his disciples for a limited time, but the Gospel had to carry on, so Jesus Christ like the Great Names knew how to **Pass the Baton** when a leader realizes the work, they have given their life too, must continue after they are gone. Therefore, they pray (successor prayer) for the next set of leaders to carry on with great success. They gladly pass the baton with grace, dignity, and love (Appendices E – Glossary and O – Pass The Baton Map).

Let's look at a few more scriptures on prayer. Philippians 4:6-7 NIV:

6) Do not be anxious about anything, but in every situation, by prayer and petition, with thanksgiving, present your requests to God. 7) And the peace of God, which transcends all understanding, will guard your hearts and your minds in Christ Jesus.

Matthew 6:33-34 NIV:

33) But seek first his kingdom and his righteousness, and all these things will be given to you as well. 34) Therefore do not worry about tomorrow, for tomorrow will worry about itself. Each day has enough trouble of its own.

1 Peter 5:7 NIV:

7) Cast all your anxiety on him because he cares for you.

So, it's clear that God should always be sought first in prayer no matter what one is facing. God knows there would be times we would be tempted to worry or be full of anxiety. He told us to pray during those times, not to worry, and trust God to help us through the situation or to deliver us out of it.

Seeking God first before we make decisions especially major decisions, marriage, buying a house, applying for certain jobs, starting a business, a business partnership, taking a vacation, etc. can help us to avoid a pattern of bad decision making. Sometimes I am guilty of making the decision without God, I'm learning to consult Him first more consistently and do my best to ask for more than one confirmation before I proceed.

Prayer is a chance to humble oneself before GOD Almighty, acknowledging that you are dependent on Father God. It's critical that we read Matt. 18:1-4 NIV: 1) At that time the disciples came to Jesus and asked, "Who, then, is the greatest in the kingdom of heaven?" 2) He called a little child to him, and placed the child among them. 3) And he said: "Truly I tell you, unless you change and become like little children, you will never enter the kingdom of heaven. 4) Therefore, whoever takes the lowly position of this child is the greatest in the kingdom of heaven."

The HUMILITY part is a very important key. Just because God says we can come boldly to his throne of grace does not mean we can come pridefully.

Hebrews 4:14-16 NIV reads 14) Therefore, since we have a great high priest who has ascended into heaven, Jesus the Son of God, let us hold firmly to the faith we profess. 15) For we do not have a high priest who is unable to empathize with our weaknesses, but we have one who has been tempted in every way, just as we are – yet he did not sin. 16) Let us then approach God's throne of grace with confidence, so that we may receive mercy and find grace to help us in our time of need.

Luke 18:9-14 NIV 9) To some who were confident of their own righteousness and looked down on everybody else, Jesus told this parable: 10) "Two men went up to the temple to pray, one a Pharisee and the other a tax collector. 11) The Pharisee stood by himself and prayed: 'God, I thank you that I am not like the other people-robbers, evildoers, adulterers – or even like this tax collector. 12) I fast twice a week and give a tenth of all I get.' 13) "But the tax collector stood at a distance. He would not even look up to heaven, but beat his breast and said, 'God, have mercy on me, a sinner.' 14) "I tell you that this man, rather than the other, went home justified before God. For all those who exalt themselves will be humbled, and those who humble themselves will be exalted."

Again, it is important – HIGHLY CRITICAL that HUMILITY is the key when we approach God in prayer and when we live our everyday lives. Is it possible that some prayers have been delayed or even denied because of a lack of humility in our approach to God and/or how we interact with and view others? With pride as rampant as it is, it's vitally important that humility shines forth when we pray – a genuine childlike faith and dependence on Father GOD.

We must understand our faith is not based on our works, but on the grace and mercy of Father God. Jesus must be Lord of our hearts; our hearts belong to Father God! Another scripture to remember is Matthew 7:21-23 NIV 21) Not everyone who says to me 'Lord, Lord', will enter the kingdom of heaven, but only the one who does the will of my Father who is heaven. 22) Many will say to me on that day, 'Lord, Lord, did we not prophesy in your name, and in your name drive out demons and perform many miracles?' 23) Then I will tell them plainly, 'I never knew you. Away from me, you evildoers!'

When we look at Matthew 15:1-9 NIV 1) Then some Pharisees and teachers of the law came to Jesus from Jerusalem and asked, 2) Why do your disciples break the tradition of the elders? They don't wash their hands before they eat! 3) Jesus replied, "And why do you break the command of God for the sake of your tradition? 4) For God said, 'Honor your father and mother' and 'Anyone who curses his father or mother is to be put to death.' 5) But you say that if anyone declares that what might have been used to help their father or mother is 'devoted to God', 6) they are not to 'honor their father or mother' with it. Thus you nullify the word of God for the sake of your tradition. 7) You hypocrites! Isaiah was right when he prophesied about you: 8) 'These people honor me with their lips, but their hearts are far from me. 9)They worship me in vain; their teachings are merely human rules.'" These scriptures show us that our mere words and deeds are not enough, GOD wants our whole heart. God must be on the throne of our hearts and allowed to lead us, especially through prayer so, there is no room for the enemy of our soul. Praying on a regular basis helps a person to stay humble.

The **Humbleness/Humility** that Jesus Christ of Nazareth must increase and become greater in our lives while we decrease (self/the flesh) become less (John 3:30). That we consistently point others toward Jesus Christ and God Almighty not towards ourselves. (See Appendix E – Glossary) It takes humility to realize that the **God Sized Calling** cannot be done in one's own strength, that even Jesus Christ and the Great Names had help with their **God Given Destiny**, they had a team or **Divine Destiny Helpers** when one prays for help, God sends people who are assigned to help the leader (praying, working, fundraising, volunteering, recruiting, etc.) His will concerning fighting for justice (helping the poor, the "Least of These", etc.) and other means of advancing the **Kingdom of God** (See Appendix E – Glossary). That **Godly Stewardship** is managing God's resources/blessings with skill, wisdom and integrity is what was required of Jesus Christ, the Great Names and all of us as well. (See Appendix E – Glossary).

God called me to write about Prayer Intercession because it is crucial that we know how to 'stand in the gap' not just for ourselves but for so many others, especially those who do not know how to pray for themselves. The book is titled, "It's Praying Time! – What You Need to Know About Prayer Intercession". God instructed me on how to make the book easy to comprehend and apply to one's life right away. It is the first book that I started, finished, and published for the glory of God. God knows we are living in times when we would have to pray without ceasing, that it would be harder to live in this world without a solid prayer life.

In "It's Praying Time! – What You Need to Know About Prayer Intercession", it's clear that the Prophet Daniel was able to endure the oppression of Babylon because he was a man of prayer, that prayed three times a day faithfully (Clayton, 2022, p.58). Even when the law said that Daniel could not pray to his God, that did not stop Daniel from his custom of praying most likely morning, afternoon, and evening. Daniel's **Faithful** prayer life with GOD Almighty caused him to be protected when he was thrown into the lions den, angels closed the lions mouths and Daniel was unharmed (Daniel 6). (See Appendix E – Glossary) A lot can be learned from Daniel. **When trouble came Daniel was ready because he didn't let his success, status, position, or influence keep him from having a faithful prayer life with GOD.**

It's my prayer that we remember that as God blesses us, we will always need Him! That is very important to keep child-like faith and humility in our relationship with GOD. It is good to remember where GOD has brought us from, there are always times when we need GOD to remember us. Prayer is not just for emergency situations, but it is a way of life, a committed lifestyle choice.

Prayer is a way to stay connected to God the Father the true source of our existence. A divine connection that should not be neglected, taken for granted or used only when a crisis arises. In this life we were told of the troubles to come (2 Timothy 3:1-9 and Matthew 24:3-14) therefore it is imperative that we continue to pray for one another, ourselves, communities, countries, and the world at large. Especially the times we live in we must continue to pray until something happens.

Defining Justice & It's Significance

Justice how does one define it? **Justice** is ensuring the oppressed, the poor, the most vulnerable are protected, provided for, and released from oppression, hatred, racism, discrimination, **Poverty**, and violence (See Appendix E – Glossary). See the Justice vs. Injustice comparison chart. The Bible references justice numerous times, especially for the poor, the orphans, the widows those who are most vulnerable in society. I think it is important to look at why that is. The scriptures often refer to GOD as the GOD of Justice! See Isaiah 30:18 NKJV "Therefore the LORD will wait, that He may be gracious to you; And therefore He will be exalted, that He may have mercy on you. For the LORD *is* a God of Justice; Blessed *are* all those who wait for Him." and Psalm 33:4-5 NKJV "For the word of the LORD is right, And all His work *is* done in truth. He loves righteousness and justice; The earth is full of the goodness of the LORD."

Even Jesus lets us know when we neglect the **"Least of These"** those who are most vulnerable, the poorest of the poor, the rejects, and outcasts of society, those who are oppressed spiritually and naturally, we have neglected Him (Jesus). The Symbolic Jesus in disguise – Matthew 25:40-45 (See Appendices E – Glossary and I – "Least of These" Map).

Justice vs Injustice Chart

JUSTICE	INJUSTICE
PEACE/HARMONY	VIOLENCE/CHAOS
RELIGIOUS FREEDOM	RELIGIOUS OPPRESSION
PROSPERITY	POVERTY
COMMUNITY POLICING	POLICE BRUTALITY
OPPORTUNITIES	DISCRIMINATION
NICE HOMES	SLUMS/GHETTOS
INTEGRATION	SEGREGATION
FAIR HOUSING	RED LINING
CIVIL RIGHTS	JIM CROW LAWS
The Great/ HUMANTARIANS	GOLIATHS/OPPRESSORS
HEALTHCARE	INADEQUATE/NO HEALTHCARE

Injustice is defined as taking advantage of the poor and oppressing them through "**Hijacking of the Faith**", religious manipulation; violations of their rights, a refusal to share wealth and other resources with the most vulnerable in society (See Appendix E – Glossary). Aren't the disenfranchised usually the ones who suffer great injustice at the hands of those who are stronger and more powerful themselves? Wouldn't they cry out to GOD for help? Yes, they would, and yes, they have. GOD has always been faithful to send help and deliverance especially to those who need it the most.

Religious Manipulators are people who deliberately take the Holy Bible out of context to oppress others by implying they are superior and the oppressed are inferior (See Appendix E – Glossary). God has consistently delivered justice to those who were in actual slavery or spiritually oppressed, in the Old Testament, New Testament and until now. Another view of justice is making sure those who have been harmed, misused, taken advantage of receive proper vindication. There are numerous synonyms, here are some: due process, honesty, integrity, law, right, truth, amends, compensation, correction, equity, evenness, justness, penalty, reasonableness, recompense, reparation, fair play, and fair treatment.

The Bible has shown many examples of not only injustices, but quality examples of justice. Once one realized how wrong he had been how there is not only a desire but an absolute conviction to pay back not only what was taken but to pay extra to show forth an effort of genuine remorse through correction, recompense, or reparation. The chief tax collector, Zacchaeus was rich and when he encountered Jesus, he no longer wanted to take advantage of people. Luke 19:8-9 KJV 8) "And Zacchaeus stood, and said unto the Lord: Behold, Lord, the half of my goods I give to the poor; and if I have taken anything from any man by false accusation, I restore him fourfold. 9) And Jesus said unto him, This day is salvation come to this house, forsomuch as he also is a son of Abraham." So surely if Zacchaeus could see how he took advantage of the poor and now pay back what he stole from them, how much more GOD will do for those who need justice as well?

Society is not short of grave and tragic injustice. We have seen GOD raise up individual and collective voices, champions, advocates who usually face great adversity to stand up against insurmountable odds, giants, or oppressors. I often hear people say where was GOD when bad things happen? It is interesting that people don't see GOD working through people who fight for JUSTICE day in and day out. They don't seem to see when these Champion Advocates **(Collaborators/Partners)** have laid down their lives–socially, mentally, emotionally, financially, familially, even physically (See Appendix E – Glossary). How can someone give so sacrificially without hardly receiving anything in return?

Jesus Christ and the Great Names were all **Called to Carry One's Cross** that although difficult one understands no cross, no crown. One must endure **Hardships** of varying levels, while partnering with GOD, to role model how to carry one's cross (**Suffer**ing/**Afflictions**) while still serving God and humanity especially in the fight for justice Mark 8:34. One of the afflictions that Jesus Christ and The Great Names of Justice have endured is being **Villainized** a tactic used by Goliaths, Oppressors, Religious Manipulators to discredit, slander, or assassinate The Great Names of Justice and the Least of These that they fight for by destroying one's reputation, image, character through various forms of propaganda so they are not believed or trusted and to try and stop their fight for justice. (See Appendices E – Glossary and S – Accomplishments vs. Afflictions)

There are clues, hints, evidence that a greater force is at work and that GREATER FORCE IS GOD ALMIGHTY! GOD is there when someone steps in and does what they are called to do and STOPS the injustice from happening. GOD is there when people refuse to turn a blind eye to wrongdoing of others and will not be silenced no matter the cost. Jesus Christ and the Great Names all had a **Righteous Indignation**, an anger that comes from the injustices that are afflicted upon the "Least of These", an anger that says, "This must be stopped!" (See Appendices E – Glossary, J – Identify Injustice Map, K – Fighting Injustice Map). Yet it's interesting when no one has stood up, that we all can see injustice for what it is. Some synonyms to injustice are wrongs, inequities, outrages, disservices, indignities, unfairness, criminal, negligence, and miscarriage of justice.

Examples of injustice are harming the innocent, sending innocent people to prison for crimes they didn't commit, overtaxing the poor, the murder of innocent people, a guilty man walks free of all charges! A blatant refusal to do what is right especially when the opportunity presents itself, to add insult to injury to know it's grossly unfair and still allow the miscarriage of justice. Over time quotes about evil and wrongdoing have surfaced that really help to expound on the issue of justice.

Martin Luther King Jr. once said, "He who passively accepts evil as much involved in it as he who helps to perpetrate it. He who accepts evil without protesting against it is really cooperating with it." (King Jr., Martin Luther; www.goodreads.com; Dec. 2022)

Albert Einstein said, "The world is a dangerous place, not because of those who do evil, but because of those who look on and do nothing." (Einstein, Albert; www.goodreads.com; Dec. 2022)

"The only thing necessary for the triumph of evil is for good men to do nothing." – Unknown (Unknown; www.goodreads.com; Dec. 2022)

Winston Churchill said, "You have enemies?" Good. That means you've stood up for something, sometime in your life." (Churchill, Winston; www.goodreads.com; Dec. 2022)

"One must stand for something, so one does not fall for anything." – Unknown. (Unknown; www.goodreads.com; Dec. 2022) Even this quote is a reminder that one can fall into allowing injustice to occur because we refuse to stand for what is right. The times we live in call for action, not inaction. If ever, there was a time to stand up for what is right, now is that time. Simply put JUSTICE WILL NOT WAIT ANY LONGER! There are those who have been preparing for this very moment, it is my prayer that when it is time to come forth, they will be ready and will not let anything, or anyone stop their fight for justice.

They will embody a true relentless pursuit of justice despite the odds, obstacles, and opposition they face, just like Jesus Christ and The Great Names of Justice. GOD is calling for a people who will be strong, courageous and help those who need justice to receive it. They knew NO JUSTICE, NO **PEACE**! (See Appendix E – Glossary) The real question is who will answer the call and stand up for JUSTICE no matter the cost? Who will not shrink back in the face of great adversity? Who are the champions that will go and get the victory for the vulnerable, downtrodden, and overlooked for GOD ALMIGHTY?

Why I Researched Prayer & Justice?

Prayer has been and continues to be a passion of mine. That prayer is more than what I can get from God but knowing the value of being able to communicate with the one that created me. I like to look at the different aspects of prayer because I know the POWER OF PRAYER WORKS! I would not have written this thesis if it wasn't for my prayer life. GOD kindly reminded me to write and finish this thesis numerous times now, who am I not to obey? As I have been praying throughout my faith journey, I have received instructions from God and carrying out those instructions have brought me to the place where I am today.

I promised GOD when I went back to school, I would go for Him. Meaning I would obtain my Biblical Degrees, Certificates, Ordinations and Licenses for His glory. Here I am towards the end of my promise to God and could not have made it this far without prayer and faith in GOD ALMIGHTY. Prayer has given me strength to keep going even when I thought I could not finish this thesis, even when I thought GOD couldn't be right in choosing me for this assignment.

There were numerous attacks, setbacks, disappointments, and heartaches that came as I set out to write this thesis. Yet, I remained faithful to my prayer life and cried out to God that he would give me strength, focus, motivation, and determination to not only start my thesis but to have a strong faith finish. In my heart I know that GOD called me to write this thesis not just for myself, but for those who have asked for more research on this topic, those who come after me, and to encourage and motivate them to keep praying even when it looks like all hope is lost.

Like Jesus Christ and the Great Names, they were not strangers to devastating **Tragedy** an intense suffering of the loss of relatives, friends, innocent children to murder or some other terrorist act, unable to see family, sickness, and disease. The heaviness of depression from things beyond one's control that are hard to understand (See Appendices E – Glossary and L – Dealing With Tragedy Map). Jesus Christ and the Great Names experienced loss of loved ones and would be very familiar with the **Kuber-Ross Grief Cycle** (Appendix E – Glossary) (Kubler-Ross, Elisabeth On Death and Dying). I can remember when tragedy or injustice of some kind would surface and couldn't be ignored; how I would cry out "Someone should do something about this! Someone stop this now!" It brings me to the poem that is usually said to remind us that at some point someone must listen, stand up, and do what GOD is calling them to do, Obedience is required.

The poem, "Everybody, Somebody, Anybody, Nobody", Author Unknown states: **Everybody, Somebody, Anybody and Nobody. There was an important job to be done and Everybody, Somebody, Anybody, and Nobody was asked to do it. Everybody was sure Somebody would do it. Anybody could have done it, but Nobody did it. Somebody got angry about that, because it was Everybody's job. Everybody thought Anybody could do it but Nobody realized that Everybody wouldn't do it. It ended up that Everybody blamed Somebody and Nobody did what Anybody could have done.**

At first, I would get such a laugh from reading this poem. As I read through with serious eyes, I realize it's the mistake myself and so many others have made. When it's time to RISE TO THE CHALLENGE, how often do we think it's someone else's responsibility to stand up against INJUSTICE? Again, this poem is a reminder to me and all of us, that we all have a part to play in standing for JUSTICE.

I know when GOD is talking to me, I can't ignore Him and I must obey what He tells me to do. I am fully aware that GOD speaks to each of us in His special way. It's up to us to obey GOD when He gives us instructions. Often what GOD asks us to do can seem impossible and even overwhelming.

Yet as I set out to prove my thesis it will be seen that GOD calls ordinary people to do extraordinary things. As GOD called The Great Names of Justice to do great exploits for Him, people often forget that these great people were ordinary, flawed, complicated people with a faithful prayer life.

GOD is the reason these people could stand and face major **GOLIATHS** and **Oppressors!** (See Appendix E – Glossary) GOD was with Jesus Christ and The Great Names of Justice and their humility to take all their cares to GOD in **Empowered Prayer** is why they could do what others would not dare.(See Appendices E –

Glossary and F – Prayer Empowerment Theory Map) No longer will GOD or prayer be left out JUSTICE and those who have stood up for it! Great **Miracles, Signs & Wonders** and **Divine Greatness** followed Jesus Christ and the Great Names because they were collaborators/partners with God Almighty, obeyed whole-heartedly through consistent humility and service to humanity. (See Appendices E – Glossary, N – Miracles, Signs & Wonders Map, P – Great Follower to Great Leader Map and Q – Path to Greatness Map).

I am endeavoring to encourage others to answer GOD's call on their lives. That IT IS TIME TO FINISH what GOD is calling you to do. A reminder that if God can empower me to stand and face great odds through prayer and obedience, then so can you! This is a loving and kind nudge that there's a reason you can't stop thinking about writing that book, play, tv show, movie, starting that business, running for government office, being an advocate for the oppressed, accepting the call to ministry, etc.

God knows what He has placed on the inside of you and it's **Birthing Out** season where God has blessed each person with a calling, assignments, a destiny – yet it must be prayed out through seeking God and following His instructions to bring them into existence, to complete the calling, the assignment and fulfill one's God Given Destiny (See Appendix E – Glossary). It's TIME TO PUSH (P.U.S.H. PRAY UNTIL SOMETHING HAPPENS) AND GIVE IT ALL YOU GOT! Think of the times you worked hard at your job, churches, ministries, raising a family, obtaining your education, serving The Least of These, etc. You put the hours in, right? Now it's time to do the same for GOD and yourself. It takes a higher level of commitment and sacrifice to achieve what GOD is calling you to do.

A reminder that Jesus Christ and the Great Names all experienced the **Garden of Gethsemane Prayer (Moment)** when Jesus wrestled with the agony of being crucified, yet he **Surrender**ed to God's will. When a person is faced with the agonizing choice of continuing to obey God or quitting, yet they choose to carry on just like Jesus did. "God's will be done." = A higher level of surrendering and partnering with God Almighty (Matthew 26:42) (See Appendix E – Glossary). It's my prayer that as you read my thesis it will motivate you to commit and prioritize birthing out what GOD placed on the inside of you.

Through empowered prayer I wrote the It's Praying Time Series: What You Need to Know About Prayer Intercession, Soul Winning, Humility Is Required, No More Idols, Obedience Is Required, Chapter 44 in Called to Intercede Volume 1 – Jesus Prayed and Still Does, and An Intercessor's Pain – none of those books would be possible without Father GOD, Jesus Christ, or the Holy Spirit. It took a lot of prayer, faith, and surrendering to God's will to birth those books out. I am glad to share that I learned to sit at the Lord's feet to share my concerns and frustrations with Him, but most importantly to receive my marching orders (instructions) for that day. GOD desires my partnership, and I desire His partnership, for I know I can't accomplish what I need to without GOD ALMIGHTY.

Like Jesus Christ and the Great Names, I have been through a **Wilderness Preparation & Testing** where God leads the person who said yes, into an intense season of equipping, training, and building. God does this to test the person's heart to see if they will still obey Him in the toughest of circumstances and will they allow this season to humble them. The humility process is again a reminder that it is not about them, but about GOD and the person's dependency on GOD. Deuteronomy 8:2 (See Appendices E – Glossary, P – Great Follower to Great Leader Map and Q -

Path to Greatness Map). My process won't look exactly like someone else's, but GOD knows how to get the results He is looking for. I had to decrease so Jesus Christ could increase in me (John 3:30). I pray Philippians 4:13 NKJV on a regular basis, "I can do all things through Christ who strengthens me." As I desire to do **Greater Works** and mighty exploits for Father God (John 14:12 & Daniel 11:32) I understand that I must choose to humble myself, because pride and GOD do not mix. (See Appendix E – Glossary)

It's important to have leaders that identify injustice but fight for justice or against injustice as well (See Appendices J – Identify Injustice Map & K -Fighting Injustice Map). Otherwise, the issue of the Everybody, Somebody, Anybody, Nobody poem continues, when we have the power to be the Ones that GOD is calling us to be, and the world so desperately needs right now. **Will you be the answer to someone's prayer?** It's my prayer that as you read this thesis that you will come to this realization that **you are the answer to someone's prayer**.

.

Chapter 2 – The Prayer & Justice Connection

Introduction

This thesis aims to prove that prayer is the foundation for justice, therefore it was important to analyze the connection between prayer and justice through the current research available. The link between prayer and justice is not new at all and there are various sources and materials on the topic of prayer and justice. The main two arguments that surfaced as I compiled my research that pertained to prayer and justice were:

1. **Arguments for the Prayer & Justice Connection.**
2. **Arguments against the Prayer & Justice Connection.**

As I analyzed the research and what those in the fight for justice are saying and experiencing it will be clear how important prayer is in the fight for justice and the misunderstandings that some have about prayer.

My thesis is adding new and authentic research to the areas of prayer and justice through the lens of the Prayer Empowerment Theory, observations, content analysis of six great names prayer lives: Ruby Bridges, Mother Teresa, Coretta Scott King, Martin Luther King Jr., Nelson Mandela, and Desmond Tutu. My research includes several credible published books, documentaries, museum exhibits, movies, articles and surveys on prayer and justice, that I drew conclusions from.

Scope & Research Gap

Most of the existing research on prayer focuses on prayer and healing, prayer as medicine, if prayer works, how often people pray, and the benefits of prayer. The current research has been divided; some studies have shown prayer works, heals, and provides great benefits to one's mind, body and soul. The other side says prayer does not work and does not heal anyone, yet these same studies say that prayer has been proven to be a comfort and considerable source of strength for those who do pray. My thesis will not expound on some of these arguments directly, because the focus of my scope is that prayer works even when it may take longer or is not answered in the manner that one was expecting it to be.

I found research on arguments for and against justice. For the sake of keeping my thesis focused on its topic, I will not expound on those arguments. However, I couldn't find extensive detailed research that explored the connection between prayer and justice through surveys, research testing, substantiated facts in academic format that would be harder to challenge or discredit. Millions of dollars have gone into prayer and healing research. I did not find any major financial investment in prayer and justice research; however, this is a start in that direction.

Arguments for the Prayer & Justice Connection

In The Black Church documentary, Henry Louis Gates Jr. explores the history of prayer and justice in the Black Church. **From slavery to the civil rights movement to current day justice movements, the consensus is that prayer and action is what brings about justice.** (Gates, *The Black Church Documentary*, 2021)

In "Prayer and the Inner Life in the Struggle for Justice" a presentation on prayer and justice, Mr. Brandon L. Paradise is aware that prayer made the difference in the Civil Rights Movement. He sees the need for more research on prayer, justice, prayer transformation individually and socially. (Paradise, 2021). Paradise states:

"- "This presentation at the 2021 conference of the Institute for Eastern Christian Studies reflects on the significance of prayer in the struggle for justice."

"The presentation concludes with the suggestion that Orthodox thinkers further develop connections between prayer and social justice, especially through examining the African-American civil rights movement for insights that may further expand and enrich Orthodox thought on prayer and collective life."

"..for many Christians in America, prayer is not understood as an existentially transformative, purifying practice with the capacity to produce individual and social transformation."

"…King maintained that Christian love actively comes to the aid of anyone who is in need."

This presentation helps to prove my thesis through qualitative means of observing Dr. Martin Luther King Jr.'s prayer life, the Civil Rights Movement and his push for non-violence to bring social justice to the United States of America.

Gates and Paradise overall have the same conclusion that prayer was the transformative practice, tool that helped individuals through slavery, the Civil Rights movement and even current day justice movements. Both Gates and Paradise have a thorough understanding that prayer and action were major components of not only the fight for justice, but what it really means to be a Kingdom believer. A Kingdom believer does not just pray only or fight justice only but understands there is a beautiful union between prayer and action that serves as the foundation for the justice movements of old and new. I agree with both Gates and Paradise's research that, disciples or kingdom believers faith is one that utilizes prayer effectively to bring Heaven to earth through God's justice, not just mere man's justice.

Of the books I reviewed that support my thesis they all had various insights and additional perspectives that I had not considered before. According to John Crossan in his book, The Greatest Prayer – Rediscovering the Revolutionary Message of THE LORD'S PRAYER, "On the one hand, since God is a God of justice, you cannot pray to such a God in a state of injustice—not at least, without insincerity or even hypocrisy. On the other hand, to pray sincerely and with integrity to such a God risks empowerment by that God for the same justice."(Crossan, 2010, p.20)

Crossan stated, to develop spiritual maturity, an individual must move beyond prayer requests to prayers of empowerment. "You have been waiting for God, he said, while God has been waiting for you. No wonder nothing is happening. You want God's intervention, he said, while God wants your collaboration. God's kingdom is here, but only insofar as you accept it, enter it, live it, and thereby establish." (Crossan, 2010, p.89-90)

That the Lord's Prayer is so much more radical than we have been giving it credit for. I agree with Crossan that God is the God of justice, and the Bible mentions specifically those who need help and special love attention from Him through Kingdom Believers (Jesus Christ's disciples):

"The poor and needy - in a rich society, Widows and orphans - in a patriarchal society and Resident aliens - in a tribal society" (Crossan, 2010, p.44)

Crossan goes on to argue that it's not Godly stewardship to simply pray and not work for or help the most vulnerable in society. Crossan consistently states that we do not ever see a "one-sided coin" with just prayer on one side, or justice on one side; that it is just not possible to have one without the other. **Crossan even explored that the Bible is talking about distributive justice (sharing everything fairly) more so than retributive justice (judicial punishment) only.** I believe the Bible is talking about a more compassionate balance between distributive and retributive justice, which is known currently as social and restorative justice.

Prayer and justice work complimentarily together and the next book that I researched explains why. Tony Campolo and Mary Albert Darling authors of "The GOD of Intimacy and ACTION stated:

- "..and unless these local congregations are also equipping their people to work for justice issues, especially on behalf of any who are poor and oppressed, they are failing to live out biblical mandates, and their religious lives could become narcissistic." (Campolo, 2007, p.15)

- "Fully devoted followers of Christ...involves commitment to what Jesus was committed to: maintaining a deep, mystical connection to God that empowered him to be compassionately connected to others, particularly the outcasts of society." (Campolo, 2007, p.15)

- "But the third (doing justice) is optional for far too many of us; and even those who see its value may still think it is a calling for others, not for them. Dorr, however, contends that none is optional, and Mary and I agree. These are not components from which we pick and choose. To do that is to distort the Christian faith." (Donal Dorr author of Spirituality and Justice) "..Paul was so adamant when he said in Ephesians 4:1, "live a life worthy of the calling you have received" (NIV). (Campolo, 2007, p.18, 21)

Campolo explains that the Kingdom of God has four basic consequences:
1. "An awareness that Christ is in the poor and oppressed, waiting to be loved and served.

2. A call to challenge institutionalized religion

3. An understanding of the importance of entering into one another's sufferings

4. A plan for the world as it should be" (Campolo, 2007, p.41)

Campolo points out, "The wrong use of religion must be challenged." "True Christianity works to liberate oppressed people and heal oppressed creation, not to legitimize their oppression." "The Holy Spirit,...empower(s) people to break the chains of oppression by enabling them to see..how evil the oppressors really are." (Campolo, 2007, p.42)

"One of Jesus Christ's major purposes was to advance the Kingdom of God here on earth, through empowered prayer and action." (Campolo, 2007, p.45) "**Jesus was the ultimate prophet.** He came into the world declaring **that a new kingdom was breaking loose** in history, and that **we should pray and work for its realization.** Jesus' life, death, and resurrection were all designed to provide the means for creating God's Kingdom here on Earth." (Campolo, 2007, p.45) **"Prophets of God give birth to justice movements, and the gates of hell cannot prevail against them."** (Campolo, 2007, p.45)

Mary Darling is aware of the power of Christ "Centering Prayer", sitting quietly before God's presence can bring. Darling emphasized the benefits of centered prayer as focusing less on us, living more holistic lives and being strengthened through the Holy Spirit to do Jesus' work. Darling stated:

- "Yet these times of silence can result in us living a more holistic gospel by helping us find the inner peace in Christ that equips us to bring peace to others." (Darling, 2007, p.132)

- "When we cultivate this kind of silence, we gradually focus less on ourselves." (Darling, 2007, p.133)

- "When we wait for God by yielding in silence to God's Spirit within us,…we will have the strength we need to do Jesus' work." (Darling, 2007, p.145)

Darling's friend, **"Paul, who is heavily involved in justice issues, puts it simply: "If you want to work for justice, first get on your knees."** (Darling, 2007, p.182) I couldn't agree more with Paul and even more so with Darling's understanding that prayer happens first and through, **"The Holy Spirit…must empower what we do. Without that spiritual dynamic we can do nothing that will have any lasting significance for the Kingdom of God."** (Darling, 2007, p.192)

In "Faith-Based Organizations (FBO) in Transnational Peacebuilding" by Tanya B. Schwarz; she researched three different faith-based organizations, and how they used prayer. Each organization focuses on different types of social injustices yet all of them use prayer in various formats from quiet meditation, verbal prayer, prayer conferences, written prayers and prayer songs too. The consensus was prayer was a very vital aspect in the fight for justice for those who need it the most.

In fact, one worker that use to work for a different social justice organization with no emphasis on prayer burnt out after a few years and had to leave that position. She was glad that prayer was a major focal point in her current International Justice Mission position, which has helped her to avoid depression and burnout. Schwarz captured in her research that prayer helped to strengthen FBO workers to continue to carry on since they worked with very difficult cases of human rights violations, demanding workloads and even traumatic experiences. Some FBO workers who were interviewed made it clear that if it was not for prayer individually and corporately, they could not continue in this type of important yet intense and life-changing work. Schwarz captured that prayer helped to strengthen them to keep going even with challenging work cases. (Schwarz, 2018, p.90)

Schwarz's important research has helped to substantiate my thesis, "The founder, Gary Haugen of International Justice Mission (IJM) began with prayer, and he solicited at least 100 people to pray for him or he wouldn't start it." (Schwarz, 2018, p.86) And he understands the importance of having that continued support system of prayer to keep IJM going. Schwarz stated in the conclusion of her research, "For instance, I revealed the critical role of prayer in peacebuilding – in FBO contexts, as well as in their on-the-ground projects." (Schwarz, 2018, p.190)

In Melinda M. Johnson's thesis, "Building Bridges: Church Women United and Social Reform Work Across the Mid-Twentieth Century" she lays out the history of Church Women United (CWU) over the centuries CWU saw injustices and started with prayer. Prayer moved CWU to action for children and women both locally, nationally, internationally, and politically. **CWU wouldn't stand for a false religion that allowed oppression, poverty, and discrimination of others because of their race or faith.** Prayer was used as empowerment that birthed out World Day of Prayer, Peace Day, a Nobel Peace Prize, and substantial offerings to help the most vulnerable. Johnson noted the following:

- "...women in these interdenominational associations have attacked specific problems by focusing first on concentrated prayer and then moving forward with action." (Johnson, 2015, p.28)

- "The committee's first major initiative was to ask members to pray every Sunday evening for an hour." (Johnson, 2015, p.32)

- "Rooted in the early communal prayer groups of missionary units around the country, this was a powerful method for connecting women, and out of it eventually emerged the World Day of Prayer..." (Johnson, 2015, p.32)

- "Communal prayers, the women believed, would bolster their efforts to improve the lives of women and children around the world." (Johnson, 2015, p.32)

- "They viewed war as a man-made effort to eradicate God's gifts on earth, and believed instead in the power of prayer and love of one's enemies." (Johnson, 2015, p.57)

- "Therefore Asian, Latino, African, Native and European Americans were all equals in the eyes of God and needed their assistance to ensure that all were treated equally for that was the biblical directive around which they organized." (Johnson, 2015, p.101)

In Rearticulating Religious Rhetoric, a thesis by Annie K Kelvie, she researched how the Community United Church of Christ (CUCC) used prayer throughout their service, Bible study and outreach ministries. Kelvie observed how the CUCC's book club, The Pub Theologians would pray and read social justice books to help them with ideas to consistently fight for justice. One of the Pub Theologians leader, "Michael developed a specific prayer to identify and feel the sufferings of others. Then the prayer was a push to do more than just listen and throw money at the problem, but to become involved in social justice causes/issues." (Kelvie, 2020, p.172-173)

Kelvie succinctly described how prayer can be used verbally, written and digitally to stir people to see racism, unfair incarceration as the sins they are, sympathize with those who have been victimized, and be motivated to lasting committed action against social injustices. "Church members then engage with, transform, and push back against these emotioned rules as they create and share compositions of their own that combine their faith with civic engagement toward greater social justice." (Kelvie, 2020, p.173-186)

As I researched further, I came across "A Six-Week Study Guide for THE GREATEST PRAYER by Dominic Crossan" prepared by Jeanne Zammataro and the United Church of Christ Economic Justice League. This six-week study guide really correlates with Dr. Annie K Kelvie's thesis where the Pub Theologians took time to study relevant books on social justice and then came up with reflective questions and prayers that would motivate committed action to help the poor, oppressed and most vulnerable in society. This study guide helps one to see that prayer and justice go together and that the church must speak out on these issues.

It was important to me to include organizations that saw the troubling times we live in and how they combine prayer and action to address those various injustices. Prayer & Action - Joining Together to Become Part of the Solution to Gun Violence in this Country is one such community that is standing up to stop gun violence in America through unified prayer and action to achieve sensible gun laws can be enacted to help keep children and others safer in this country. Prayers & Action's activism is very similar to those great names who refused to stand by and do nothing. The way they use guided prayers, petitions and call on government officials shows that those prayers have helped to propel them to stand up against gun violence in this country and invite others to join them: https://prayersandaction.com/survivor-sunday-resource-kit/

"The mission of Survivor Sunday is to remind our country that compassion for the survivors of gun violence is rooted in Jesus' parable of the Good Samaritan (Luke 10:25-37). Jesus commanded us to love our neighbors, which includes strangers, and anyone caught in the crossfire of violence, regardless of their faith, ethnicity or neighborhood."

Both Prayer & Action and Prayer and Action Coalition share the same fundamental stance, values and goals of Church Women United that no matter one's racial identity, faith, or status in life that all are equal in the eyes of God and deserved to be treated fairly in all aspects of their lives. And that there is a lot of prayer and work to be done to help those who are most impacted by injustice.

Prayer and Action Coalition Biblical Principles for Just Policies in Policing and Criminal Justice has focused on: Mourning the loss of Breonna Taylor, George Floyd, and so many others who were lost to racialized violence (police brutality). They believe in praying and standing up against injustice, and are committed to changing laws at all levels to bring justice to all. They see everyone as the human being God says they are.

https://ministrywatch.com/evangelical-groups-launch-police-reform-initiative/

"The organizations and leaders that make up the Prayer and Action Justice Initiative believe prayer and protest should lead to concrete policy action at the federal, state and local levels. While each jurisdiction is different, there are biblical principles that can be applied across the board."

"We believe that can change through transformative faith-based prison programs, teaching of life and work skills, and a restorative re-integration into society that reflects the God-given dignity of every person."

"On election day and every day after, we are invited to respond to God's call to do justice and love our neighbor through prayer and by working for the well-being of our political community."

Prayers and Action Coalition activism can be found in these systemic steps of:

1. Endorse Biblical Justice and Race Statement

2. Assemble and Pray

3. Act (Unified Social Impact)

4. Give

Another Bible study on justice, "Justice and the Gospel" by IJM/CRU(Campus Crusade For Christ) layouts that Jesus came to set the captives free from oppression and injustice, therefore the Christian believer has a duty to do the same. If we would read the scriptures on justice and humble ourselves enough to fight for justice. "While on earth, Jesus brought rescue to the physically and spiritually oppressed. He also prepared the way for His final coming, which will bring all that is awry into order. **Redeemed by Christ, it is the responsibility of the church to seek justice until He returns.**"

IJM/CRU's stance on Biblical justice and how to carry it authenticates my thesis that it takes personal reflection questions that one ponders within and with God. **If one is not challenged to be like Jesus through prayer and reading scriptures and meditating upon them, then how can one achieve it?** Again the point about serving with humility shows up throughout this Bible study of Jesus and Justice.

I came across several articles or blogs that further reinforced my research and even added additional insights. Susan Rakoczy wrote the blogpost titled, "Prayer or Action? The Tension Explored" which explored that **people could make the mistake of doing activism without (praying) a spiritual foundation or think their faith is personal and does not require them to live out standing up against injustice.** The reality is both prayer and action are needed to bring justice to the poor, oppressed and most vulnerable.

"Our God is a God of justice and peace and we come to know God both in prayer and in concrete action toward justice, peace, and the care of creation." "In the life of Jesus as given to us in the Gospel witness we see no choice between prayer or his mission of liberation. Rather, we see the integration of these two dimensions of life." "This call to contemporary Christians throughout the world is to learn how to do this: to grow simultaneously in the life of prayer and in commitment to social transformation, to walk on the two feet of love of God and love of neighbor." (Rakoczy, 2023)

Susan Rakoczy has a unique gift and writing ability that encourages one to pray and be committed to social justice. The loving reminder that one can have a deep prayer life, but should not ignore the issues and problems of the current times. **She has a beautiful way of reminding us to do like Jesus did, that we should not separate prayer from our liberation mission. To sum it up we are the answer to someone prayers, and even sometimes the answer to our personal prayers.**

Nicole Spector wrote the online article "This is Your Brain on Prayer and Meditation on BETTER by Today NBC News Online". Spector shows that when trouble and stress come people usually want to do something, and some turn to prayer even if they aren't particularly religious. Prayer helped Alcohol Anonymous members to avoid cravings and temptation, MRI scans of their brains showed how prayer helped the cravings to go away, helped people to relax and to be calm even in fight or flight situations. **There was a push for a balance between prayer and action.**

"The key, Dr. Hokemeyer finds, is largely one of balance. **"The trick to balancing prayer with results is to recognize when is the time to pray/meditate and when is the time to go out and do something,"** says Hokemeyer. "One of the purposes of prayer and meditation is to regain our footing so that we can step out into the world and take positive action: we reconnect, re-center, recharge and **gain the strength necessary to take steps that will create real change. In other words, prayer is the fuel that lights the fire of action**." Dr. Anna Yusim, a psychiatrist and the author of "Fulfilled: How the Science of Spirituality Can Help You Live a Happier, More Meaningful Life," strongly recommends prayer and meditation, deeming them "wonderful and powerful tools," but ones that are made all the more wonderful and powerful "when coupled with concerted action." Nicole Spector's article lends a hand to my thesis that prayer helps one to leap into action when it's time. That merely praying is not enough, that there is a time to pray and act. Nicole Spector considers herself agnostic, but she felt a need to help after the Parkland, FL school shooting and even after she helped a lot, she was led to pray." (Spector, 2017)

Piercarlo Valdesolo journal article, Scientists Find One Source of Prayer's Power – Communing with a higher power increases self-control demonstrates how people draw strength from God through praying because it's a social connection, and people draw strength from one another as they interact with each other not just a supernatural one since atheist benefited it too. **That those who pray have more will power to resist temptation, wrong decisions, and have the fortitude to keep going in the right direction**. "The religious find strength through God; this we know. But a new study conducted by Prof. Malt Friese and Michaela Wanke suggests that even non-believers can get in on the action. In a forthcoming issue of the Journal of Experimental Social Psychology, they present evidence showing how and why prayer might increase anyone's ability to resist temptation. The authors ground their study of prayer's power in something called the "strength model" of self-control. The strength model suggests that our cognitive resources, like our physical resources, are limited. **We run out of gas.** So, how do we replenish these cognitive resources, or even increase our cognitive "endurance"? "..but the scientists here proposed that prayer might be another means through which individuals protect themselves from breakdowns of will."

Participants who were asked to pray about a topic of their choosing for five minutes showed significantly better performance on the stroop task after emotion suppression, compared to participants who were simply asked to think about a topic of their choosing. And this effect held regardless of whether participants identified as religious (70 percent) or not. This does not rule out the possibility that prayer has other effects on resisting temptation, and the spiritually inclined could see the hand of God as another causal factor here. But as the holidays approach, it reminds us all of where we derive so much of our day-to-day strength. Interacting and connecting with the people around us." (Valdesolo, 2013)

Piercarlo Valdesolo article strengthens my thesis in two underlying points that **people draw strength from God when they pray and the right people (quality support system/divine destiny helpers) motivates us to achieve what does not seem possible. The right social connection encourages us not to give up.**

Frank Fincham wrote the journal article, "What Can Science Say About the Study of Prayer? Separating Fact From Fiction in the Templeton Prayer Study". Frank Fincham does a great job of pointing out that the largest research study on prayer is not the final conclusion on how intercessory prayer works or not.

He points out that there has been other intercessory prayer research done in various areas including married couples vs. infidelity, the comforts that one feels knowing others are praying, good health benefits on the person actually interceding for someone else. He stated that no matter the results those on the side of science or theology would still have challenges or explanations for why certain results turned out that way. The largest prayer study is known as Study of the Therapeutic Effects of Intercessory Prayer (STEP) and aka "The Templeton Prayer Study". **"Intercessory prayer may be complex, but it can be scientifically shown to be effective provided we take seriously Mahatma Gandhi's observation that "Properly understood and applied, [prayer] is the most potent instrument of action."** From the beginning it could have been foreseen that research on distant intercessory prayer was unlikely to resolve either scientific or theological debates on its effects." (Fincham)

Fincham enhances my thesis again especially with the quote from Gandhi. That prayer is an instrument of action, when one prays action is produced; one has the strength, courage and will power to face even the most dangerous odds to fight for justice for all.

Kristen Rogers wrote the online newspaper article, "The psychological benefits of prayer: What science says about the mind-soul connection." Rogers pointed out how many Americans turned to prayer during the pandemic, even those who were not religious or hardly ever prayed. Scientists and psychologists claim it's hard to study and do experiments on research; some even feel that no quality research study exists (although there have been many). It pointed out how skeptical some scientists and some psychologists are about prayer. It was interesting to hear from a Christian woman who has been a believer for more than 40 years trusted in God no matter what the outcome would be concerning her husband who had been hospitalized for COVID-19. (Rogers, 2020)

"During Rob's stay, Carol felt alone, sad, concerned and feared the unknown. As a faithful Christian for more than 40 years, she turned to praying to God and meditating upon Bible scriptures. "I think that it probably encouraged me," Carol said. "It calmed me at moments. ... **I think it centered me back again and reminded me that I was not in charge**." Carol prayed alone and with family, mostly on her knees in deference or while walking. The goal wasn't to change God's mind, Carol said. "God was in control of this before it happened." **The purpose was to surrender her own desires and align herself with God to hear whatever he had to say. "I know it's a two-way conversation**," she said. "I really felt the peace of God telling me that I wasn't even supposed to worry about that. So, I did not worry. I'm usually a planner, but I knew that God had a plan." Carol and Rob credited prayer as one of the factors that led to his recovery. Rob is back home now, recuperating.

The Kochons aren't the only people who have prayed over pandemic related outcomes. In March, the Pew Research Center reported that in a survey, 55% of US adults said they had prayed for an end to the spread of coronavirus. Large majorities of Americans generally and US Christians specifically who pray daily have turned to prayer during the outbreak. But so did some who seldom or never pray, and people who didn't belong to any religion have started praying." (Rogers, 2020)

Rogers emphasized my thesis that prayer has been used to face challenges that one cannot face in their own strength. That it takes humility to know that life can be too much at times and we simply cannot control everything that happens, yet with the power of prayer, we can face it even when we are fearful, hurting, grieving and don't know what to do.

Prayer Requires Action a blogpost by Mari-Anna Stalnacke & Flowing Faith shows the importance of prayer and action together. That to accomplish what God is calling one to do, it takes prayer and it's not wise to go about doing such great tasks without prayer. **Stalnacke, debunks that Christians just pray only, that we are called to be doers of God's word.**

"Recently, I heard someone saying, 'Christians are stupid when they think prayer changes things.' He thought Christians only pray and do nothing. But that's not the way prayer works. Praying does not mean we sit on our hands the rest of the time. It's not an excuse to do nothing. We are to go forward in faith. **First, we pray as it all depended on God, then we work as everything depended on us. Because prayer requires action.** The beautiful thing about prayer is the fact it invites God's power to change things within us and around us. And when we look at our lives with the eyes of faith, we start to see the little ways how prayer changes things. **People start to get along, we get empowered to love our enemies** or things just happen at the right time. Prayer is a welcome mat for God to be involved in our affairs. It's an invitation for God to create something beautiful out of the ashes of our lives. **We pray hard and then we do everything in our power to be part of the answer.** God has not called us to be passive. **He's called us to be his partners. Only when we are active participants in God's work, we are truly living out our faith**. So, no matter what do not despair. Instead, pray and then start doing the next thing that is worth doing. God's Spirit will guide your steps while he is working behind the scenes. So, prayer changes things, for sure. Sometimes miracles occur, yes. **But most often we are called to be the change we are praying for.**" (Stalnacke, 2021)

Stalnacke validates my thesis that prayer catapults Christians to leap into action by faith. She does an excellent job of debunking the criticism and stereotype that believers just pray only. It showed how many believers in the last few years see that we must pray and act courageously.

Prayer Is Where The Action Is a blogpost by David Ledford, argues that prayer is action, prayer is not just words. That we are called to pray for the veterans and help them too. That Jesus was not a fan of long repetitious prayer and that prayer is not about being seen in public praying. "On the front of the shirt, there is a quote from John Wesley who said, "prayer is where the action is". It's true that prayer shouldn't just be a to-do list that we give God. And while it is ok to pray for our own needs, it is also important to pray for others. **The kind of prayer Jesus liked the most was a simple prayer that simply connected you or the people around you with God and with those in need**. Yes, prayer doesn't have to include words. That's exactly what John Wesley said. Prayer is about action. God wants our loving actions more than our words. **Instead of "what prayer can I say", let's ask ourselves "what prayer can I do"**. (Ledford, 2021) Ledford authenticates my thesis that prayer is not just merely words but are indeed actions that must be carried out. **The connection that prayer is not just thinking someone else will do it but knowing that one has the power to change things too.**

Faith Research's report, "Thinking of Jesus Motivates Us to Help Others But It May Depend on Your Faith" key argument is, When we think of Jesus, we are motivated to help others. "If you need a little boost in motivation to help others, thinking about Jesus might just give you the boost you need. But of course, despite these findings, you'll still need to put these motivations into action.

Actively look for ways to help others, even in small ways. There is surely no shortage of help needed in this world." (Faith Research) This survey report sheds light on my underlying thesis that the great names studied all looked to Jesus as motivation and inspiration to do their greater works. So, I'm not surprised at the results of this survey. Many of us have never met, yet we are all drawing and coming to the same conclusion this is a fact that cannot be denied, ignored, or simply brushed off as mere coincidence: that empowered prayer leads to action that brings real meaningful change, especially justice to those who need it most.

Arguments Against the Prayer & Justice Connection

So, let's say for argument's sake that I took the opposing viewpoint that prayer does not change the outcome to justice (not the start of justice). I would have a very hard time proving that point since my research has shown that those who are non-believers, atheists and agnostics even admit that they pray when trouble arises, tragedies and grave injustices occur, and they help where they can through activism, fundraising, and other ways. My research consistently demonstrated that prayer is not just empty words, but a divine connection to be empowered by Almighty God to move into action and accomplish greater works in the fight for justice. That those who have tried to do social justice work without praying, usually do not last long because of the amount of stress, pressure and opposition associated with this type of work is shown in Schwarz's valuable research in *Faith-Based Organizations in Transnational Peacebuilding*.

The research showed those who argue that prayer does not change outcomes concerning justice usually have a misunderstanding on how prayer really works. It's clear that they think that Jesus's disciples or kingdom believers (Christians) just pray and expect God to make everything happen. Those who have a deeper and more mature understanding of prayer realize that's not how it works. Those who misunderstand how prayer works cannot see the connection between prayer and justice. Yet, I argue just because you cannot see the link between prayer and justice does not mean it is not there and does not work. Since justice work is truly God's work and we are collaborative partners with Him, it's clear that God has designed justice work that we must rely on Him through empowered prayer and faith. It would be very unwise to approach justice activism/work as a regular nine to five type job where you hardly need to pray to get the work done.

The misunderstanding of how prayer really works could stem from observing well-meaning individuals who consistently pray about social injustice issues but hardly ever put any real action behind their prayers. It's important not to make exaggerated generalizations that apply to all, based on well-intended people and a lack of understanding. The Presidential Prayer Team (PPT) conducted a two-dimensional survey in April 2020 on the profile of American's prayer lives. The survey produced various results, but the consensus was that most American's prayed during the pandemic, to build a relationship with God, to talk to God, to get help during a crisis, to influence God's actions, to increase peace and reduce anxiety, a way or worshiping God, and **one way God transforms you**.

Yet, it was clear from the survey results that Americans do not agree on exactly how prayer works, therefore it is clear that this is an area of interpretation to many. Even the 14% of people surveyed stated they were not certain if God answered prayers and weren't sure how he answers prayers. The survey showed that younger people tended to not see the value in prayer and could be missing out on what has helped some of the Great Names for centuries now. (Missions Box, 2020, "Most Americans Pray But Disagree About How Prayer Works."). I must admit I know young people, middle aged people and older people who do not take prayer seriously either. Again, I say just because someone does not know how prayer works or devalues it, doesn't mean it does not work.

When one does not understand that prayer is not a one-way street or a monologue, it truly is a two-way street or a collaborative dialogue. So, if someone observes a person that just prays, gives a list of requests and does not wait and listen for God's response and instructions, does not actively "watch" for God's answered prayer, and does not even know what he or she should be doing to bring about justice, it can become easy to see how one is disillusioned with prayer and it's connection with justice. Yet, the key to improve the understanding of how prayer works is to acknowledge the different types of prayer and the process of prayer, See Appendices F – The Prayer Empowerment Theory Map, G – The Prayer Transformation Map, H – Acknowledges God Map, M – Obedience Map and E – Glossary. After reviewing those concept/process maps and the Prayer Empowerment Theory terms and definitions, it makes it easier to understand how prayer works, especially through prayer transformation, prayer empowerment theory and the obedience map. Keeping in mind God is a God of order, structure and stability, so what we put into our personal relationship is what we get out of it. If one is open to humbling and surrendering oneself to God's divine instructions, there really is no limit to the greater works that can be accomplished for His glory.

Another misconception that prayer does not change anything in the fight for justice and even the argument that prayer does not work at all stems from what is perceived as unanswered prayers. I'm not surprised at individuals who are disheartened with prayer because a loved one died, when they believed God to heal them. Or when some have experienced praying for a particular job, promotion, scholarships, spouse, children, healing, house, etc. and they did not get what they wanted. A person's faith will be tested throughout his or her life and if the faith level is only based on prayers being answered exactly the way one wants it, then one will be disappointed at some point in time. I can understand how heart breaking this can be, especially when one has prayed and seen God answer prayers through miracles that could not be explained, now this time there is no miracle. Even in the fight for justice one's faith will be tested and when prayers are not answered the way one prayed that does not mean prayer does not work.

When civil rights activists, innocent children and youth are murdered during peaceful protests in the fight against injustice, these are tragedies that are hard to understand. It can open the door to so many questions, why was this allowed to happen? Where was God? Why weren't my prayers answered? Unfortunately, if one is not careful bitterness can be allowed to come in and take root. It is during these times that one must rely on Jesus Christ and their faith in Him to get through difficult times and experiences. The six great names I researched all dealt with various levels of tragedies and disappointments during their fights for justice. Yet, they did not let tragedies hinder or stop their faith in God or what He called them to do that helped so many others. The Dealing With Tragedy Map (Appendix L) shows the process that the six great names all went through. It serves as a reminder that the six Great Names were called to greatness (See Path to Greatness Map – Appendix Q) therefore they would not understand why certain things happened, but they still trusted God and continued to pray even when the outcomes weren't what they wanted.

It's important to point out with "unanswered prayer" or prayers that did not get answered the way one thought it should, that emotionalism is not faith. As one matures and grows in their faith walk with God it becomes clear that one's emotions are not the basis of one's faith and prayers. Those who have lived their lives based on their emotions usually do not accomplish all that they have set out to do. Yet, those who learned that their emotions do not dictate their faith, or prayer lives see a greater outcome in their faith walk and the goals they accomplish.

As I studied the six Great Names prayer lives and their lives in general it was clear that they did not allow their emotions to rule them. All of them faced great fear, anxiety, anger, depression, sadness, and grief yet they did not allow those strong and very real emotions to stop them from doing the greater works and fulfilling their God given destinies. It was during those times of fear and various emotions that they prayed to God for strength to keep going, courage to keep fighting and wisdom on how to keep fighting for justice. The six Great Names trusted God no matter what they faced or what the outcome would be, they understood what it meant for God to always be there for them.

Another issue that arises with arguments against prayer and justice working some are disappointed with the length of time that it takes for prayers to be answered. Some have questioned and challenged why it took so long for slavery to end, for civil rights to be enacted, Jim Crow Laws to be dismantled, apartheid to be abolished, improvement in the education system, improvement for housing, improvement in the criminal justice system, enacting and enforcing laws against human trafficking, etc.? Especially those who did not live long enough to see change come their frustrations are valid, however it does not mean that prayer does not work in the fight for justice when it takes longer than expected. Humanity having to respect that God is sovereign and He truly has the final say has been a struggle for some time now; that God's timing and agenda are according to His schedule not necessarily ours. I observed the six Great Names all had that in common, knowing that they were merely His servants carrying out God's will for their lives and trusted God's timing concerning manifested prayers.

Conclusion

As I researched it showed that those who fought for justice (against injustice) consistently were the people of faith. It was clear to me that God was a God of justice, therefore He raises up champions of the faith that pray and seek His guidance on a daily basis. Therefore, God's servant leaders are at the forefront in empowered prayer that propelled them to fight for justice even when the

God-sized calling seemed impossible. Almighty God has a system of checks and balances that usually His ministry leaders, servant leaders, The Great Names, churches and organizations that have a solid prayer life and were determined to obey the call of God with urgency, efficiency and excellence; are the ones that stand up to corrupt laws, oppressive and abusive governments, religious institutions/leaders that "hijack the faith" through religious manipulation, and corrupt world leaders. The Great Names understood that faith without works is dead, and it's simply not possible to fight justice with a dead faith, therefore they were empowered through prayer to fight for justice and achieve what was deemed impossible.

    As I evaluated the research, I concluded that the arguments and evidence for prayer being the starting point (foundation) to justice far outweigh the arguments against it. I could understand why some have disagreed with how prayer works, however I stand firmly on that prayer works even when we can't understand every nuance, detail or timing of it. Even with the six Great Names that I tested, as I researched additional Great Names, like Harriet Tubman, Abraham Lincoln, Moses, Frederick Douglass, Sojourner Truth, Al Sharpton all had/have a prayer life and utilized that prayer life to catapult them into action in their fights for justice. On another note, God gave me this thesis assignment so the world can see how important prayer is, and that Prayer is the Foundation for Justice for the Great Names, churches, organizations and for all who are willing to partner and collaborate with God through prayer and obedient action.

Chapter 3 – The Prayer Empowerment Theory

The Prayer Empowerment Theory

I could have used Servant Leader, Transformational or even Critical Race Theory. However, as I am determined to prove my thesis those theories don't show a valid connection between prayer and justice. As I launch out into the deep through prayer and obedience to God, I see a new theory emerge, **The Prayer Empowerment Theory**. (See Appendices E – Glossary & F – Prayer Empowerment Theory Map) Those who embrace advancing the Kingdom of GOD here on earth, know prayer is empowerment by GOD Almighty to do His perfected will. Their submitted lifestyle, obedience and humility to GOD make them great partners/collaborators with Him.

Before they were GREAT, THEY PRAYED FIRST! When God revealed what His plan was to the Great Names, it was overwhelming, yet it caused them to seek GOD even more. Their faith was strengthened if GOD said it, they trusted Him. Even when their lives were threatened, fear didn't stop them, they prayed for courage and strength to continue. Even when enemies attacked them, their families, and others, the Great Names had the humility and compassion to forgive and offer reconciliation.

They continued to pray daily because they faced impossible odds without GOD's help. As they prayed GOD empowered them to fight against injustice. Prayer is the main ingredient in their success and often overlooked. Their faith was lived out in courageous actions, directed by GOD Almighty. The "GREAT NAMES" knew prayer and empowered action went together to fight against injustice, that it was a continual partnership to advance the Kingdom of GOD.

Research Steps

1. Brainstormed numerous Great Names, prayed and sought God for the most feasible names to start with and God made it clear to start with Ruby Bridges, Mother Teresa, Coretta Scott King, Martin Luther King Jr., Nelson Mandela and Desmond Tutu.

2. Gathered autobiographies, biographies, documentaries, articles, etc. that discussed their prayer lives, fight for justice, accomplishments, struggles, childhood, etc. through the Milwaukee Public Library, Google Scholar, EBSCO, Stanford Search Works, JSTOR, OpenThesis, etc.

3. Took extensive handwritten notes as I researched each of the six Great Names.

4. Researched existing books, doctoral dissertations, journals, research studies, etc. on the connection between prayer and justice used the same search engines/databases from Step 1.

5. Kept track of my literature review material in an excel spreadsheet provided by GradCoach YouTube Channel that I summarized notes, quotes, the type of material, etc. Included the material that was most credible and relevant that proved my thesis.

6. Researched theoretical frameworks and realized that all my research was done, and I did not have a theoretical or conceptual framework to support my thesis.

7. Researched the Servant Leader Theory, Critical Race Theory and Transformational (Leader) Theory and noticed these theories did not explore the connection between prayer and justice, or any other theoretical or conceptual framework.

8. Researched and found this journal article on the importance of the Theoretical Framework Grant, Cynthia & Azadeh, Osanloo. 2014. "Understanding, Selecting and Integrating A Theoretical Framework in Dissertation Research: Creating the Blueprint for Your "House"." *Administrative Issues Journal* 4, no. 2 (2014): 12-26.

9. I trusted, prayed and asked God for help in Jesus Christ name, and He gave me the Prayer Empowerment Theory and Conceptual Frameworks.

10. Hand wrote what God gave me for the Prayer Empowerment Theory in a notebook and drew the Concept maps, wrote the Glossary as God revealed patterns, repeating words and/or concepts.

11. After I had the theory and concept maps, prayed to God on what else should be included: compiled the Six Great Names Prayers and their highlights of Accomplishments vs Afflictions.

Content Analysis Methodology

To prove my thesis, I utilized Content Analysis of six individuals: Ruby Bridges, Mother Teresa, Coretta Scott King, Martin Luther King Jr., Nelson Mandela, and Desmond Tutu. Five out of six are now deceased, and I could not interview them directly. For consistency, Ruby Bridges was handled in the same manner as the rest. My analysis was explicit, but some was implicit where I inferred what else was being said in the text. There is some bias because of my own assumptions, knowledge, and background.

I used Content Analysis & Questionnaire Methodology to focus my analysis on their prayer lives and justice in the following areas: (See Appendices A – E)

- Who were they praying too?
- How often did they pray?
- Why were they praying?
- What were the outcomes of those prayers?
- Were others aware of their prayer lives, and what did they observe?
- What were my additional observations of their prayer lives?
- What were their views on justice and injustice?
- What was their spiritual foundation, what was their faith based on?
- Who and what did they draw strength from?
- Who were their inspirations, who did they admire?
- Why did they fight for justice?
- Was prayer used as a substitute for action?
- Why did they continue to fight for justice?
- What did "The Great" all have in common?
- What are they most remembered for?
- What are their greatest accomplishments?
- What obstacles did they face along the way, how did they overcome them?

I depended on the research, interviews, and views of others in biographies, Internet articles, blogs, etc. to complete a quality analysis. I had several names on my brainstorming list, however after much prayer the six names that stood out for my research was Ruby Bridges, Mother Teresa, Coretta Scott King, Martin Luther King Jr., Nelson Mandela and Desmond Tutu. My sample size of six is small for testing the Prayer Empowerment Theory, however with the amount of research, analyzing and synthesizing it, I will prove my thesis with this small sample size. Humans are prone to error that is a limitation of myself and the research material. Therefore, it was crucial that I found credible sources who were either the individuals and/or confidants authorized to write their autobiographies and biographies.

The Prayer Empowerment Theory Concept Maps

The Prayer Empowerment Theory is comprised of various Concept Maps that show that Prayer is the Foundation for Justice, and what the six Great Names experienced on their prayer journey to greatness. After compiling and analyzing my research through Content Analysis it was important to detail the processes, systematic steps that the six Great Names experienced throughout their lives in visual format.

See Appendices F-Q that shows the various Concept Maps:

1. The Prayer Empowerment Map – Shows the process of the Prayer Empowerment Theory.

2. Prayer Transformation Map – Shows the stages/levels of prayer that the Great and those who partner with God go through to advance the Kingdom of God.

3. Acknowledges God Map – Shows how The Great acknowledged God from an early age and throughout their lives, demonstrating gracious humility.

4. Least of These Map – Shows how The Great had a heart for the Least of These.

5. Identify Injustice Map – Shows how The Great knew what injustice was.

6. Fighting Injustice Map – Shows how The Great fought against injustice through prayer and empowered action.

7. Dealing with Tragedy Map – Shows how The Great handled tragedy by being better and shows how others handled tragedy through bitterness.

8. Obedience Map – Shows how The Great obeyed God's instructions and the benefits for doing so, and the criticism they face for their obedience as well.

9. Miracles, Signs & Wonders Map – Shows how The Great experienced numerous miracles, signs and wonders because of their obedience, humility and faithful prayer life.

10. Pass the Baton Map – Shows how The Great prepare, train, and pray for the next generation of leaders to continue the God Sized Calling.

11. Great Follower to Great Leader Map – Shows how The Great, were once great followers which helped them to become great leaders.

12. Path to Greatness Map – Shows how The Great pray throughout their process and embark on the journey of greatness.

I could have written out these systematic steps, but being an Alverno Alum my Alverno education kicks in for me. I understand that people learn and comprehend in various ways: reading, writing, observing, hands-on doing, listening and a combination thereof.

The Prayer Empowerment Theory Glossary

The Prayer Empowerment Theory consists of 55 terms with definitions. Many of the terms are not complicated, and I wrote it that way on purpose. I prayed a lot during this prayer thesis that I would be able to birth this assignment out successfully and in a way that brings God the glory. Yet, I understood that some people that read this thesis may not be familiar with Biblical and spiritual terminology. So, the goal was to make it comprehendible. As I researched and synthesize the information there were patterns, repeated terms and concepts of terms that I had to include in the glossary.

Since God gave me the Prayer Empowerment Theory as a special assignment, it was important that I build this theory out as much as possible. I truly wanted to lay a solid foundation for the Prayer Empowerment Theory where it would be understandable, replicable and applicable. I was determined to utilize the Prayer Empowerment Theory throughout my thesis and understood that a robust glossary would help the readers, students, researchers, etc. to have a better understanding of: what this thesis was about, that I proved that Prayer is the Foundation for Justice and that it would help people to embrace prayer, improve their personal relationship with Jesus Christ, learn something new and know that sometimes you are the answer to someone's prayer and sometimes your own.

The Six Great Names Prayers & Accomplishments vs Afflictions

After I did a thorough Content Analysis of the six Great Names Prayer lives it was prudent that I include at least one prayer that each Great Name prayed. (See Appendix R – Six Great Names Prayers) I believe it adds validity to the fact that each of the six Great Names valued prayer, their prayer lives and prayed first before they set out to do any of the greater works that God had preordained for them to do. Their prayers also provided a glimpse into their prayer lives, faith and trust they place in God Almighty. In addition to that I chose prayers that the six Great Names were known to have prayed, that carries more weight that others around them not only knew about their prayer lives but were aware of these specific prayers. These were not the only prayers that they prayed but it was still important to include at least one prayer from each Great Name to show the significance that they placed on prayer and their prayer lives.

After synthesizing the research of the six Great Names, the research consistently showed miraculous accomplishments and intense afflictions (See Appendix S – Accomplishments vs Afflictions). I learned that those who endeavor to partner with God Almighty will experience great highs and lows. Yet, it was important to show summarized highlights of accomplishments and afflictions for each of the six Great Names. The evidence was overwhelming that God's hand was definitely upon the Great Names lives and their prayer lives helped to produce amazing results that could not be ignored or debunked. The Accomplishments vs Afflictions helps to prove my thesis for the amazing accomplishments that each experienced, but also for the intense afflictions that they experienced as well. Greatness is not simply defined by just the good and amazing awards, rewards, accolades, accomplishments; it is also defined by those painful tragedies, heart-breaking moments, betrayals, etc. that could only be overcome through the power of Jesus Christ and a solid prayer life. Especially in the fight for justice, those who keep praying and have others praying for them can endure hardships like good soldiers of Jesus Christ and keep going with their God-given assignments, tasks and fulfill their God-given destinies.

Another point to make here is as seen in the Prayer Empowerment Theory Concept Map that **there's a balance between what one accomplishes for God Almighty and what one endures for God Almighty**. God's justice work is designed that we humble ourselves and depend totally on Him. The six Great Names knew it was not humanly possible to accomplish or endure all that God had in store for them, but knew to start, continue and always end with empowered prayer. Even when one knows that humility is the key, it is something about intense afflictions that help to ensure that one stays humble, that one must keep praying. The Great Names usually don't have a choice about being publicly displayed before the world, that is why it is very important that they demonstrate a solid prayer life and gracious humility. God doesn't mind people being Great, after all it is Him that is making them Great, but God and prayer will not be forgotten, ignored or dismissed any longer. Part of my assignment with this prayer thesis was to make it clear that God must get the GLORY, that He is the reason that the Great Names could accomplish what others could not. The Great Names had a solid foundation in Jesus Christ and in prayer.

Questionnaire Testing Methodology

The Prayer Empowerment Theory was tested through four core outlines, that all help to prove that Prayer is the Foundation for Justice. For consistency all four of the core outlines were changed into nine dichotomous questions (Yes or No format) for testing. I picked the dichotomous format because it is straightforward, simple and easy to summarize results. I understand that since there were only two options it could be viewed as limiting, however for the purposes I was setting out to achieve it suited the research, testing, summarizing and substantiating the thesis's ultimate goal. Also, the dichotomous format is known to produce more accurate and precise results and since The Prayer Empowerment Theory is being introduced, I know it was important to present detailed testing that could be replicated in future research, experiments and studies.

After I completed my research of all six Great Names it was important to present evidence that was easy to understand and proved that Prayer is the Foundation for Justice. I was determined to show qualitative evidence as seen in Chapter 4 – The Prayer Lives of Six Great Names through direct and indirect quotes, and quantitative evidence as seen in Chapter 5 Summary & Conclusion and Appendices A – D.

The Prayer Empowerment Theory Four Core Outlines

The Prayer Empowerment Theory Outline

1. She or he prayed first, (usually a silent Jesus Christ Centered Prayer)
2. God spoke to them on what they were to do for Him in the fight for justice.
3. She or he obeyed God wholeheartedly.
4. Had a heart for the "least of these".
5. Endured intense hardships, afflictions.
6. Continued their prayer life.
7. Sacrificed so others could live a better life.
8. Achieved what was deemed IMPOSSIBLE.
9. Left a legacy that still inspires and lives on to this day.

See Appendix A for the Prayer Empowerment Theory Questionnaire Testing.

The Prayer Foundation Outline

1. She or he prayed first.
2. She or he prayed daily.
3. Prayed throughout the day.
4. She or he asked God for help.
5. She or he valued their prayer life.
6. Saw prayer as a foundation to justice.
7. Used prayer and action to fight for justice.
8. She or he had faith (kept faith) in Jesus Christ.
9. She or he stated (viewed) Jesus Christ as a key role model.

See Appendix B for the Prayer Foundation Questionnaire Testing.

The Fight for Justice Outline

1. God directed she or he (through prayer).

2. She or he knew what injustice was.

3. She or he knew what justice was.

4. She or he cared for the "least of these".

5. She or he faced great adversity.

6. She or he knew God's calling.

7. There was a cost to fight for justice.

8. She or he is considered an Activist.

9. She or he made a difference.

See Appendix C for the Fight for Justice Outline Questionnaire Testing.

The Prayer Outcome Outline

1. She or he asked God for help.

2. God sent help.

3. She or he asked God for strength.

4. She or he asked God for courage.

5. She or he asked God for insights.

6. She or he endured and overcame.

7. She or he received award/honors.

8. She or he achieved greater works.

9. She or he left a (lasting) legacy.

See Appendix D for the Prayer Outcome Questionnaire Testing.

Evaluation of The Methodologies

The Content Analysis provided an insightful analysis of the connection between prayer and justice from several aspects that included the Theory, Concept Maps, Glossary, Six Great Names Prayers and Accomplishments vs Afflictions. Since I am laying a foundation for the Prayer Empowerment Theory it was important to provide qualitative data that was comprehendible, reliable and practical. My thesis aims were to prove the connection between prayer and justice, but to present the Prayer Empowerment Theory in a way that was logical, distinguishable, and applicable. I think it was important to have the Prayer Empowerment Theory in word format, outlines, concept maps, comparison tables, terms and definitions and dichotomous testing results so even if that was all someone read, they would be able to understand the theory and the principles of how it works and comes together.

It's no coincidence that the Concept Maps are interconnected or overlap one another in several ways. The Prayer Empowerment Theory is simple to grasp, yet, has intricate layers within it that is shown in the four Core Outlines/ Questionnaires, Concept Maps, Glossary, Six Great Names Prayers, and Accomplishment vs. Afflictions all help to prove that prayer is the foundation for justice and that the Prayer Empowerment Theory is legitimate in its claim of that very fact.

Even the four Core Outlines of the Prayer Empowerment Theory proved to be essential in the detailed testing portion of my research. It was important to have the qualitative data, but just as important to have quantitative data that supported my thesis. As I prayed to God Almighty how can I test this theory in a simplistic but credible way? He showed me how to take the four Core Outlines and turn them into dichotomous questions. Then I could summarize those results into quantitative data that was concise and measurable. I trusted God to help me write the outlines in a clear manner and to turn them into testable questions that proved my thesis. The testing could be replicated for the six Great Names in my sample and to other Great Names that were not included in my sample.

The four Core Outlines of the Prayer Empowerment Theory strengthened the validity of prayer being the foundation for justice because they were testable and yielded provable results. I knew how important it was for my thesis to be supported with quality evidence through factual results.

The 55 terms and definitions in the Glossary adds credibility to the Prayer Empowerment Theory, and it's the average size for a theoretical framework. The Glossary helps to bridge a gap between the theory and the six Great Names prayer lives and journey to greatness. God helped me to see patterns, terms and concepts that were repeated in all six Great Names prayer lives and journey to greatness.

I could have used just quantitative analysis, but that would show a limited perspective on the Prayer Empowerment Theory. The Content Analysis and Questionnaire Methodology was the best approach for accomplishing and substantiating my research, analysis, detailed testing and summary of results. Content Analysis is open to interpretation and could be biased. However, I presented solid evidence for each of the six Great Names that was consistently unbiased through direct and indirect quotes, detailed testing, Accomplishments vs Afflictions, and Concept Maps that prayer is the foundation for justice.

Chapter 4 – The Prayer Lives of Six Great Names

Ruby Bridges

As I researched Ruby Bridges, I am reminded of when myself and young daughter, Elise watched Disney's movie, "Ruby Bridges" in the Fall of 2020. As we watched closely, we were able to see that not only did Ruby's parents have a spiritual foundation in Jesus Christ and God, so did Ruby! I was amazed at her mom's spiritual authority; her daughter was being shown through prayer you can conquer fear, gain strength to stand in the midst of great adversity, and accomplish what is said to be impossible.

In The Story of Ruby Bridges, "Ruby's parents were proud that their daughter had been chosen to take part in an important event in American history. They went to church. We sat there and prayed to God," Ruby's mother said, "that we'd all be strong and we'd have courage and we'd get through any trouble; and Ruby would be a good girl and she'd hold her head up high and be a credit to her own people and a credit to all the American people. "We prayed long and we prayed hard." (Coles, 1995, p.6) The fact that Dr. Robert Coles is a child psychiatrist and did not omit Ruby and her family's prayer life and faith in God is a testament to what he witnessed in them and learned from Ruby's teacher.

On the first day when Ruby and her mother left the school a protestor had a coffin with a black doll in it. "…it was the scariest thing she had ever seen." (Magoon, 2021, p.20) Even when Ruby experienced stress and nightmares her mom reminded her to pray. "Did you say your prayers before you went to sleep?"

she would ask. If I hadn't Mama would say, "Honey, that's why you're having a bad dream. Go back now, and say your prayers." "I would do as she said, and then I would sleep." (Bridges, 1999, p.48)

"Somehow it always worked. Kneeling at the side of my bed and talking to the Lord made everything okay. My mother and our pastor always said you have to pray for your enemies and people who do you wrong, and that's what I did." (Bridges, 1999, p.48) Not only did the protestor have the sign about poisoning Ruby, "One woman screamed at me, "I'm going to poison you. I'll find a way." She made the same threat every morning." (Bridges, 1999, p.22) Yet the brave Ruby went to school every morning! Even though her appetite was impacted she did not let that stop her.

"Sometimes I'd look at her and wonder how she did it," said Miss Hurley (Mrs. Henry). "How she went by those mobs and sat here all by herself an yet seemed so relaxed and comfortable." (Coles, 1995, p.14) One day Mrs. Henry saw Ruby stop and talk to the angry mob, and was curious about what Ruby was saying. Mrs. Henry asked Ruby what she said to the angry crowd. Ruby insisted she wasn't talking to the crowd. "I was praying. I was praying for them." Every morning, Ruby had stopped a few blocks away from school to say a prayer for the people who hated her. This morning she forgot until she was already in the middle of the angry mob."" (Coles, 1995, p.21)

Ruby, her family and Mrs. Barbara Henry suffered threats of violence and other consequences along the way. "Even her teacher suffered: for the bold act of teaching Ruby, she was fired at the end of the year." (Easton, 2018) Ruby's dad was fired from the job he had, white-owned stores would not let Ruby's mother shop there and Ruby's neighbors took turns guarding her home to protect them from those who might break in.

'Mrs. Henry said, "It was important to keep going." (Magoon, 2021, p.25) Through Ruby's courage to integrate William Frantz Elementary School as the first Black student she helped to manifest Dr. Martin Luther King Jr.'s dream that he ended up losing his life for.

Prayer gave Ruby not only the strength to stand for justice, and the HUMILITY to forgive those who were angry with her and threatening her. And to ask God to forgive them for they knew not what they were doing. That's what Jesus prayed on the cross at Calvary as they crucified and mocked Him.

Ruby Bridges, This Is Your Time, encourages young people but really all of us in words so beautifully said, "You only need a heart full of grace. Really, it is that love and grace for one another that will heal this world, allows us to see one another as brothers and sisters, allow us to respect the many ways God has made all of us unique and will allow us to turn our stumbling blocks into stepping stones. Stepping-stones toward the America we know we can be. United, one nation under God, indivisible, with liberty and justice for all."(Bridges, 2020, p.46, 48)

Bridges in This Is Your Time states, "The spirit of Reverend Dr. Martin Luther King, Jr. continues to inspire all those who work for peace and justice." (Bridges, 2020, p.44) Even in the loss of her son Craig, she has not allowed that to stop her, she encourages the new leaders (passing the baton) with this, "The struggle continues…May my past, my story, inspire you. The first steps toward change are never easy. Keep your eyes on the prize." (Bridges, 2020, p.52, 54)

In Through My Eyes by Ruby Bridges she shares her spiritual background and how it helped her when she was six years old and still to this day. "My mother brought us up to believe that God is always there to protect us. She taught us there is a power we can pray to anytime, anyplace. How did I get through 1960 and the long year of integration? I think it was a combination of things. For one, I really believed as a child that praying could get me through anything. I still believe that." (Bridges, 1999, p.56) Bridges humility shines forth like gold as she was dependent on God through prayer as a six year old and until now.

In Through My Eyes, "People are touched by the story of the black child who was so alone. Interest in the story keeps growing, and I'm not the one making it happen. In all of this I feel my part is just to trust in the Lord and step out of the way." (Bridges, 1999, p.60) Ruby shares how she is walking by faith, holding onto her faith and is at peace with, her life's work of "integration". For over twenty-five years Ruby Bridges has stood up against racism by speaking to students all over the world.

Ruby shared with Dr. Robert Coles perspective on her experience, "I knew I was just Ruby," she told me once, in retrospect, "just Ruby trying to go to school,…But I guess I also knew I was the Ruby who had to do it-go into that school and stay there no matter what those people said, standing outside…" (Bridges, 1999, p.47)

Ruby was awarded an honorary deputy federal marshal in Washington DC ceremony in 2000. "The marshals were still grateful for and impressed by the courage Ruby had shown years before as a first grader." (Magoon, 2021, p.37) A statute of Ruby Bridges at six years old was placed in front of William Frantz Elementary in 2014. This is a reminder that regardless of one's age or gender prayer serves as a foundation to justice. Ruby's start wasn't with being selected to integrate, it started with her faith and her family's faith in God Almighty in prayer. Ruby achieved what seemed very impossible, without significant mental trauma and emotional scarring because of prayer empowerment.

Mother Teresa

Even as I studied Mother Teresa it was amazing to see that she too prayed and meditated on what God would have her to do. Prayer was a precious communication between Mother Teresa and GOD, and that she sought GOD first through prayer. In the book, Mother Teresa Beyond the Image Anne Sebba states,

- "Meditating on these contradictions and the future direction of her life, she come to a decision. But describes the process rather differently, as 'a call within a call'. "This is how it happened,' she told her spiritual director, Priest Julien Henry. 'I was traveling to Darjeeling by train, when I heard the voice of God.'...'I was sure it was God's voice. I was certain that He was calling me. The message was clear I must leave the convent to help the poor by living among them. This was a command, something to be done, something definite. I knew where I had to be. But I did not know how to get there.'" (Sebba, 1997, p.46)

Mother Teresa's humility shined forth in such a way that it could not be ignored.

- "If Mother Teresa is, as she maintains, 'simply a pencil in God's hands', she is at once both more humble than an ordinary nun and yet also much more powerful than any world leader.'" (Sebba, 1997, p.47)

- In I loved Jesus in the Night Teresa of Calcutta – A Secret Revealed by Paul Murray, Mother Teresa experienced the intensity of dying to herself daily and carrying her cross like so many others who have dared to give God a certified yes day in and day out.

- "The fact that Mother Teresa kept saying 'yes' and allowed herself to be stretched far beyond what a person can humanly endure, helps to explain why, though consumed by the love of God, she would often ask people to pray for her, and not only lay helpers, religious sisters and priests, but also the poorest of the poor whom she served." (Murray, 2008, p.90)

- Although a very devout woman of prayer Mother Teresa still humbly asked others to pray for her, especially to continue in the work that

God had called her too. Mother Teresa is an excellent example of how prayer was that foundation to the justice she carried out daily, even when it was hard on her physical health and weighed heavy on her soul.

- "It's astounding how Mother Teresa did not enjoy the spotlight. "In Mother Teresa's case, the fact that, for years, she was the object of fascinated and insistent attention by the world's media was an affliction she found particularly difficult to bear." (Murray, 2008, p.27)

Mother Teresa similar to Coretta Scott King and Martin Luther King Jr. was someone who prayed and then got up and carried out the greater works for her Lord Jesus Christ. Sebba stated:

- "'What stunned everyone was her energy and efficiency. She saw the problem, fell to her knees and prayed for a few seconds and then she was rattling off a list of supplies she needed -...the blind, the deaf, the insane and the spastics tend to be forgotten when they need help the most. Mother Teresa understood that right away,' said the official."(Sebba, 1997, p.112)

- "Mother Teresa herself expressed her views quite clearly during an interview with Vatican Radio in 1980 when she explained that, for her, faith was something to be lived rather than talked about." Mother Teresa's sense of justice was deeply rooted in her love to care for the least of those, because Jesus commanded that we care for them." (Sebba, 1997, p.162)

- "Even though Mother Teresa was certain of her calling from GOD, there was opposition. Mother Teresa had to continue to pray for at least a year or more and do different assignments that would prepare her for her ULTIMATE calling. Archbishop Perier, "decided that no decision should be taken for at least a year." (Sebba, 1997, p.48)

- "In July 1948 Sister Teresa was informed that a one-year of exclaustration, which she had been praying for but had dared not ask for, had been granted." "Because of her insistence not just on leaving but on remaining vowed with the aspiration of setting up a new order she had to prove the unprovable, that this was the will of God." (Sebba, 1997, p.49)

- A pharmacist refused to help Mother Teresa, undeterred she sat there and prayed until the end of the day, the pharmacist changed his mind and gave her the medicine she needed. (Sebba, 1997, p.53)

For Mother Teresa it was clear that prayer and Jesus' mandates was a way of life for her, and essential not only for her, but the sisters who came to join the Missionaries of Charities.

- Prayer was daily part of the sisters' routine including Mother Teresa, they had early morning prayer together, afternoon prayer and reading, then evening prayers.

- This does not even include the prayers they would pray throughout the day for those they served, each other, and the overwhelming obstacles they faced as well.

- "She loves and trusts God and He has used her to accomplish miracles in Calcutta where one might be tempted to think that with so much poverty God had closed his eyes to human suffering and human dereliction." (Sebba, 1997, p.66)

- "Dudley Gardiner, 'Mother Teresa has God to help her with her planning, God to discuss her triumphs and share her disappointments. God to me is very real, don't mistake me, but I've never honestly felt a close personal relationship, which Mother Teresa enjoys.'

- "Mother Teresa's instinct was always to talk about Jesus and her faith in Jesus and to talk in a religious context on any other subject would have been, for her, a travesty." (Sebba, 1997, p.95)

- Mother Teresa said, "I had a good laugh over the Nobel Peace Prize. It will come only when Jesus thinks it is time." (Sebba, 1997, p.99)

- In "Great Names – Mother Teresa Religious Humanitarian by Anne Marie Sullivan", "Mother Teresa taught her sisters to rely on prayer for strength as she did." "She once said, "We do hard work. Prayer can support us, help us and enable us to accomplish what we must do joyously." (Sullivan, 2003, p.18)

- "...one of her own favorites saying in the Gospel: "In so far as you did this [kindness] to one of these, the least of my brethren, you did to me." Mother Teresa understood that the least of these was truly Jesus in disguise. "Thus, on two occasions, I remember once in Rome and once in Calcutta she took my hand in her hand and repeating the Gospel passage, spelt out the Gospel words on my five fingers: "You -did-it-to-me." "Then she said: 'The entire mystery of our lives is here Priest Paul, in these five words." (Murray, 2008, p.85)

- Mother Teresa was very clear in the Missionaries of Charity's Mission, "'Our object is to quench the thirst of Jesus Christ on the cross by dedicating ourselves freely to serve the poorest of the poor, according to the work and teaching of our Lord, thus announcing the Kingdom of God in a special way..Our special task will be to proclaim Jesus Christ to all peoples above all to those who are in our care.'" (Sebba, 1997, p.55)

When Robert McNamara wrote in support of Mother Teresa's Nobel Peace Prize nomination: (paraphrased) "That Mother Teresa's work conveys the message that genuine peace arises when there is a social order where individuals treat one another with justice and compassion. That her concern for the poor shows how conflict can be alleviated, and that world peace is possible." (Sebba, 1997, p.100)

Mother Teresa's Accomplishments in partnership with GOD In the book, Mother Teresa Beyond the Image, Even in the poem "Do Good Anyway" you can see that Mother Teresa was truly betrothed/espoused to Jesus Christ. In this world even when you have done all you could to help others your will be attacked and even hated for it, yet her RELENTLESS FAITH, DETERMINATION AND PERSEVERANCE shines brightly in this poem. Her solid prayer life and the prayers of others, her humility, obedience, and faithfulness allowed her to do a lot of good in this world well before her passing on September 5th, 1997. The Life Magazine featuring Mother Teresa states that "25 years after her death there are nearly 5,000 missionary sisters spread over more than 600 locations in more than 130 countries not to mention an army of priests and lay volunteers who pitch in around the world." (Jerome, 2022,p.4)

Coretta Scott King

Coretta Scott King was a woman of prayer as well. Her roots in prayer go back to her childhood, and beyond. Her Dad led the way in praying for their family, friends and especially their enemies. Growing up in the extremely racist South, Scott King was no stranger to the harsh realities of the racism, hatred, oppression and most notably "The Jim Crow Laws". Although she was young, she knew how they were treated as blacks was not right. She admits that her earlier experiences and her dad's devotion to praying for one's enemies definitely helped her to stand up and fight for what's right.

Scott King experienced the loss of their home to arson by suspected racists. Her dad, Mr. Scott stated, "We don't have time to cry." "He led us in prayer and told us to give thanks because we still had our lives. He even made us say we forgave those who had destroyed our home." (Scott King, 2017, p.7) At fifteen years old that was not easy for Scott King, but her dad's faithful, strong and prayerful leadership would help to set the course for the rest of her life.
Scott King always had an inner knowing that God had more for her to do, and SHE WAS RIGHT!

Coretta would marry one of the most prominent leaders of the Civil Rights Movement. What she experienced in the racist south was preparation of what was to come during the Civil Rights Movement. "After Martin's speech, carloads of angry whites surrounded the church, throwing rocks through the stained-glass windows, showering the worshippers with shards of glass. The men outside cursed and threatened to burn down the church. With rocks and curses filling the air,

Martin and the congregation prayed and sang hymns, including "We Shall Overcome." "As was our routine when Martin came home, our family filled the house with prayer and songs of praise. The climate we faced on a daily basis gave us much to pray about." (Scott King, 2017, p.99)

Scott King stated, "Still, though the future was always in our minds, we didn't have much time for long-term planning or soul searching or reflection, as there were too often more pressing matters to attend to." (Scott King, 2017, p.102) Coretta Scott King had this in common with Nelson Mandela as well who said even with all of his training some things he was daring to achieve had not been done before, that he learned as he went the momentum of things did not allow time to slow down and reflect. Scott King noticed how husband, King Jr. and other imprisoned political leaders wrote some of their best work behind bars. "There is something about the confinement, the isolation, and unjustness of those prisoners' situations that helps focus their minds on their principles. With little left to lose, their bodies already imprisoned, there is nothing left to do but state their principles unequivocally, what they will live and die for." (Scott King, 2017, p.107)

Scott King also learned from King Jr, "the value of searching for the worst cases, of allowing people to catch the spiritual dimension of their struggle and victory. The way I see it, Birmingham was so evil that only God could change it –and God did." "Never before had black people taken such unified, direct action to change the conditions of their lives." (Scott King, 2017, p. 109) Coretta Scott King said, "Although Martin never saw what his prophetic words proclaim, I was fortunate enough to see his dream come true." (Scott King, 2017, p.110)

Scott King was able to see so much momentum from the Civil Rights Movement that, "Blacks in city after city began to take the shackles off their minds, to believe what was once thought impossible: they did not have to tolerate being treated as less than human....perhaps the day was coming when they would be granted the full rights of citizenship." (Scott King, 2017, p.111)

Coretta Scott King was no exception to the painful sacrifices and consequences of standing for blacks Civil Rights in America. Scott King explains, "We talked about the many ways in which the system tried to destroy leaders. It started by trying to convince people you were a thief. This had already been attempted with Martin, and had failed. The next step was always character assassination, usually with allegations of sexual wrongdoing. If that didn't work, physical destruction followed." (Scott King, 2017, p.122). Even when Daddy King shared his struggles, "..how hard it was for him and Mama King to live with the knowledge that what Martin was doing was so dangerous. He talked about the threats the two of them endured. You don't know how it feels when a stranger calls you on the phone and tells you he wants to kill you, or kill your son." (Scott King, 2017, p.124)

Even when King Jr. would soon receive the Nobel Peace Prize a highly questionable hate filled letter showed up at King's residence. Scott King stated, "There was no question in my mind that it was prodding Martin to commit suicide. Under stress, Martin often suffered from depression. In the sick minds of those who'd sent the letter, I'm sure they thought they were pushing my husband over the edge." (Scott King, 2017, p.128)

Coretta Scott King is very forthcoming about the sorrows that her family faced from Martin's death. As she shares, "Our family had suffered so many tragedies in six short years. They kept us on our knees, praying for strength, and we found the strength to push past our pain and continue on our mission, which we had been uniquely challenged to. Sooner or later, our Comforter would come. We had to keep growing, keep building, and keep moving on." (Scott King, 2017, p.201)

Scott King is known for so many great things yet in her memoir, "My Life, My Love, My Legacy" she birthed out her "Fifth Child". Coretta stated so clearly, "Throughout out my life, whenever I didn't pray, things went badly. I would become frustrated and feel out of sync with the will and purpose of God. But whenever my life was guided by prayer, I felt good about what I was doing, and I was able to reach out to other people with love and understanding. In the wake of Martin's death, I pondered and soul-searched, trying to determine my future plans and goals, and of course I prayed. It was during this time of prayer that the idea of creating an institution dedicated to Martin's legacy rose to the top of my life's to-do list." (Scott King, 2017, p.185)

Coretta Scott King was met with a great deal of animosity and opposition as she set out to create the Martin Luther King Center. Scott King said, "Once I'd prayed about it and felt I had God's blessing, I never really doubted that I could build a great institution. I knew I could not quit. The naysayers would not stop me. When I didn't know where to look for funds, I prayed. When critics condemned me without cause, I prayed. And when the physical buildings of the Center were completed, I still prayed, thanking God for how far He had brought us and asking Him to continue His watch, to protect and guide us as we made our way forward." (Scott King, 2017, p.189)

Scott King understood the assignment and the territory that she was up against when she said, "Also I remembered that only after death was Martin so loved; while he lived, he was often condemned. Could I really have expected to be treated any differently?" (Scott King, 2017, p.190) Even with Scott King's strength, she still relied on her prayer life to carry on, when afraid, stressed or depressed. As Scott King reflects, "I did so wish for Martin during these tough moments. When he was alive, he had me. But in my crises, I did not have him to lean on. In my darkest hours, I felt so alone. I never stayed fixated on that for long though; there was too much to gain. The very fact that Martin was gone gave me a fighting spirit, encouraged me to keep building and developing." (Scott King, 2017, p.190)

Coretta Scott King faced a lot of backlash from women for being a woman, but especially for not being a "traditional woman". She recalls, "They had been taught that a woman was supposed to stay at home with the kids. I didn't fit the mold, and they didn't understand what I was doing." (Scott King, 2017, p.189) Scott King was treated with much contempt to say the least by men who once worked with her husband. "At the root of their problems with me, I think, was that I appeared to them to be a strong woman, not one to be pushed aside." (Scott King, 2017, p.190). As a woman I can relate to Coretta Scott King that this can be true that at times I have faced a great deal of opposition from women, especially women who were older than me.

Coretta did not abandon her four precious children, "the decade after Martin's death, it was of utmost importance to me to put my children first, to make sure they knew how special and loved they were. I could see the difference that this was making almost daily. I remember Martin III telling me, "Mama, a kid can live without a father, but no kid make it without a mother."(Scott King, 1997, p.213) It's clear to me that Coretta Scott King was A SUPER MOM!

Coretta achieved mind blowing success! She stated, "…when I was able to raise the millions in funds we needed, I saw that as affirmation that I'd done the right thing. When you can raise that kind of money against all odds—well, that in itself is encouraging." (Scott King, 2017,p.190)

"And by the time we completed construction in the early 1980s, we had paid it off. That in itself was a miracle." (Scott King, 2017, p.193) Like so many other great leaders, Coretta wanted children to have what she did not have as a child. "All the things I didn't have as a child, I tried to provide through the community center. I put in early-learning programs because I remembered how my lack of early training made it difficult for me to keep up in college. To see the children coming to the early-learning center was really gratifying." (Scott King, 2017, p.203) Scott King beams with joy when she says, "There were times of agony and times of joy, but there are no regrets, especially when I see what the Center means to the world." (Scott King, 2017, p. 213)

Coretta Scott King and her team had an uncanny ability to remain focused despite rumors, setbacks, character slander and so many other disheartening things that arose as she set out to birth the King Center. "We did not allow the naysayers or our own missteps to bog us down or distract us from our mission." (Scott King, 2017, p. 206) "I never expected to see so many people close to me who wanted this child of mine stillborn. Nevertheless, out of much pain and with much prayers, the King Center came forth. As with my flesh-and-blood children, I am a proud parent." (Scott King, 2017, p. 213)

Scott King was gracious and humble leader who knew, "When you are building a great institution, someone also has to help you take care of your home and your kids. I never could have done what I did without all these people."(Scott King, 2017, p.191) Coretta had a team and was grateful for them. The other angle of humility that shown forth in Coretta Scott King, just like her husband, Martin Luther

King Jr, knew that the baton would be passed. "This miraculous Center was conceived in me, and birthed by thousands of midwives—and my other children will finish raising up this sibling of theirs to independent adulthood when I'm gone." (Scott King, 2017, p. 213)

Her success was not limited to the King Center only, "Fox Theatre, where operas in Atlanta were performed, was teetering on the edge of financial collapse, I worked with local residents to save it, restore it to its original grandeur." (Scott King, 2017, p.204) Coretta Scott King and her team were instrumental in the election success of South Africa's first black President Nelson Mandela! Scott King noted that, "Charles Alphin Sr. told us that we ended up being the only American group allowed to stay. We had helped train more than three hundred thousand people to do something they had never done before: participate in a Truly democratic election." (Scott King, 2017, P.256)

To see how Scott King and the King Center could partner with the Transformation Center and other South African activist is truly remarkable, "were armed with little more than their Bibles and their faith that peaceful transition was not only necessary but achievable." (Scott King, 2017, p.255)

Coretta Scott King's prophetic and unrelenting faith had a major impact on President Nelson Mandela's election. Until I researched her, I had not known this fact in history, but ever so grateful to know it now. Scott King stated, "I had prophesied that divine intervention could not only save but also redeem South Africa. The Holy Spirit works through people. You do all you can, and then God takes over. He creates the breakthroughs in our lives that make these kinds of miraculous historical events eminently possible. When God decides a change is coming, He uses people who will be obedient to His purpose and will. Then miraculous things begin to happen. That election was powerful vindication of nonviolent resistance and its message, so often stated by Martin:

"We must either learn to live together as brothers or we perish together as fools."" (Scott King, 2017, p.257-258)

In the "In Her Own Words" internet article by Adelle M. Banks she noted Coretta saying, "The bombings, the murders, even the assassination of my husband only intensified my devotion and solidified my resolve that God had allowed me to be born at the right time in history, a time when the Spirit tracked down the willing, empowered the waiting, and magnified human outcomes far above what finite minds could conceive."

Martin Luther King Jr.

In the book "Never to Leave Us Alone – The Prayer Life of Martin Luther King Jr." by Lewis V. Baldwin it explores MLK Jr's prayer life. Mr. Baldwin states in the Preface "They reveal how King turned to prayer as the foundation of his personal spiritual life, the center of his devotional practice, and powerful sacred force in his struggle to liberate and empower people." (Baldwin, 2010, p.X) "King was arguably the most advertised religious figure in America in the 1960s, and his prayer life, philosophy of prayer, and practice of praying are immensely important for understanding him as both a person of faith and a social activist." (Baldwin, 2010, p.X)

It may not be as well-known, that when the Montgomery Improvement Association prayed first, they unanimously voted that King be the president, the leader of the movement. "It is often said that movement began with a song, but in King's case it actually began with a prayer. The date was December 5th, 1955; the scene was King's private study in his home at 309 South Jackson Street in Montgomery…" (Baldwin, 2010, p.68) "King had a face-to face encounter with what he, in the tradition of his forebears, called "A Waymaker," exposing his fears, insecurities, and vulnerabilities with sincerity and humility. Great comfort came as an "inner voice" spoke to King, reminding him that he was not alone, commanding him to "stand up" for righteousness, justice and truth, and assuring him that "lo, I will be with you, even to the end of the world.""(Baldwin, 2010, p.69)

King's call to action was indeed PRAYER, and he firmly believed that prayer led to action in order to be most effective. As King led the Civil Rights Movement his prayers were a consistent call to action.

- "In King's case prayer, voiced and unvoiced, became a call to mission or to action. He was convinced that prayer worked as an empowering and liberating force in the context of struggle." (Baldwin, 2010, p.XII)

- "He had little patience with those who turned to prayer as substitute for human initiative or who prayed while ignoring the social maladies that afflict society." (Baldwin, 2010, p.XII)

- "This is why King concentrated on persuasive prayer, or prayers of persuasion – the kind that incited listeners to action." King often reminded fellow activists that prayer was not a means to escape the responsibility and duty to stand up against oppression, hatred, racism and poverty but to keep fighting for justice, freedom and equality. (Baldwin, 2010, p.XII)

- "Carter maintains that King taught the people of Montgomery the weapon of prayer was ultimately more powerful and effective than any gun or bomb, a message they, due to "a deep tradition of Christian stoicism". (Baldwin, 2010, p.75)

King's private prayer life afforded him a great deal of strength, courage, obedience, and endurance to continue even when all odds seemed to be against him. He knew the power of prayer and used it privately even more so.

- "It is also about those moments of sacred stillness, of solitude and private prayer, when King found the courage to follow God's will and not his own." (Baldwin, 2017, p.XII)

- "Moreover, it highlights King's ability to rise above the doubts and fears that haunted him and to subvert nagging concerns about his own safety in favor of an ethic of risk, sacrifice, and redemptive suffering." (Baldwin, 2017, p.XII)

- "Evidently, King's emphasis on private prayer as creative energy was, as the content of this work shows, consistent with his tendency to place spiritual transformation at the center of every action he took as a crusader for freedom, justice, and human dignity." (Baldwin, 2017, p.XII)

- "Thus, he was able to confront the relentless pressure of the forces of evil and retrogression without faltering." (Baldwin, 2017, p.XII)

- "I am even more convinced that prayer is an enormously powerful force, which often yields what might otherwise appear impossible or unattainable to the human imagination." (Baldwin, 2017, p.XVIII)

- "As far as King was concerned, he was involved in essentially "a spiritual movement" and not simply a struggle for equal rights, social justice, and peace; this invariably meant that prayer and praying, much like the spiritual discipline of nonviolence, had to be for him a daily activity and total way of life." (Baldwin, 2017, p.68)

King was very familiar with how much suffering he and those who stood with him would have to face and endure, while fighting against injustice. King drew great inspiration and strength from Jesus Christ's prayer life and took great strides to emulate it in his own prayer life. King often identified with Jesus Christ in the Garden of Gethsemane in prayers and sermons and his loving ability to love his enemies and truly forgive them from the heart.

- "Jesus's submission prayer in the Garden Gethsemane, "Father if thou be willing let this cup pass from me; nevertheless not my will, but thine be done."; and Jesus's intercession from his cross, "Father forgive them for they know not what they do."; all became Martin Luther King Jr's personal prayers and reflected King's view of the "nature of the human condition, the power of love, and the bitter suffering that awaits those determined to transform and redeem society." (Baldwin, 2017, p.2)

- "King prayed for the strength and wisdom needed for the continuing journey through the Egypt of slavery, the wilderness of segregation, toward the promised land of freedom, justice and equality of opportunity." (Baldwin, 2010, p.21)

King demonstrated humility and visionary foresight by:

- Studying history and found that a consistent solid prayer life was important to men and women everywhere. (Baldwin, 2010, p.4)

- Knowing that the civil rights movement was not merely about himself but, "to keep his own leadership in "true perspective", to see that he was merely "a symbol" of the movement and not the movement itself…" (Baldwin, 2010, p.73)

- Thinking of leadership candidates who could carry the Civil Rights Movement forward after he was gone. (Scott King, 2017, p.126)

- Gave his wife, Coretta Scott King encouragement and credit for her strength that helped him to carry on even in the toughest and darkest of times. (Scott King, 2017, p.190)

Martin Luther King Jr. is certainly no stranger to assassination attempts and death threats, yet he did not let that stop him from fighting for civil rights, voting rights, and fair wages for the working class. GOD undoubtedly raised MLK Jr. up for that time, so in this time we all live out his "I Have A Dream Speech".

Nelson Mandela (Mandiba)

As I researched Nelson Mandela his prayer life helped him with the great losses and sacrifices in his fight against injustice. It bothered Mandela that he could not do more for his family, he had a very deep desire to take really good care of them.

- "Even when at times I am plagued with an uneasy conscience I have to acknowledge that my whole heart commitment to the liberation of our people gives meaning to life and yields for me a sense of national pride and real you. This feeling has been multiplied a hundred times by the knowledge that right up to her last letter she wrote me shorty before her death, my mother encouraged me in my beliefs and in fighting for them."

- Mandela's mother and his oldest son both died while he was behind bars, and he was not allowed to attend their funerals.

- Nelson Mandela is famously known for his Rivonia Trial Speech on April 20th, 1964, "During my lifetime I have dedicated myself to this struggle of the African people. I have fought against White domination, and I have fought against Black domination. I have cherished the ideal of a democratic and free society in which all persons live together in harmony and with equal opportunities. It is an ideal which I hope to live for and to achieve. But if needs be, it is an ideal for which I am prepared to die." It's important to remember that Mandela and colleagues were facing the death penalty. (Mandela, 2010, p.121-122)

- "Mandela became an international symbol of the struggles for justice. He was without doubt the most famous prisoner in the world. A prisoner ready by 1990, on his release, to stride across a global stage." (Mandela, 2010)

Mandela often credited the Methodist institutions he and others attended that helped to birth out the resistance movement to the apartheid oppression.

In the Spiritual Mandela by Dennis Cruywagen,

- "But witnessing such poverty on a daily basis, and experiencing it himself, affected Mandela's perceptions of black society. Studying the Bible at school and church meant that he was well aware of the Christian concept that all people were created equally in the eyes of God." (Cruywagen, 2018, p.53)

- "Religious organizations also played a key role in exposing apartheid for what it was a fraud and heresy. It was encouraging to hear of the God who did not tolerate oppression, but who stood with the oppressed." (Cruywagen, 2018, p.158)

- Mandela speech at the Methodist Annual Conference, "By your fearless commitment to truth and justice the Methodist Church and other religious bodies helped realize this. But all government, no matter how democratic, need constructive criticism and advice. I ask you to continue to play your prophetic roles, always seeking to hold the nation and all its leaders to the highest standards of integrity and service." (Mandela, 2010, p.XX)

- In addition to that prayer was not a foreign concept to Mandela. His Mother clung to her Methodist faith and prayer was very important to her, so much so that Mandela remembered that about her from his youth and drew from her example. Mandela's mother cherished her Methodist faith and prayer was very important to her, and her prayer life left a valuable impression on him. (Cruywagen, 2018, p.40)

Even Nelson Mandela could see that his college education truly failed to prepare him for his greater calling in life. In Conversations with Myself, Nelson Mandela stated, "The average teacher had fought shy of topics like racial oppression, lack of opportunity for the black man and the numerous indignities to which he is subjected in his daily life. None had ever briefed me on how we would finally remove the evils of colour prejudice, the books I should read in this connection and the political organizations I should join if I wanted to be part of disciplined freedom movement. I had to learn all these things by mere chance and through trial and error." (Mandela, 2010, p.27)

However, he did not let that stop him, turns out his cultural traditions in being prepared to be a Chief, listening to how matters and problems were discussed and solved proved to be instrumental in his fight for justice for all. In "Conversations With Myself", "I have always tried to bring people together, you know?' (Mandela, 2010, p.XX)

Mandela used the power of prayer and fasting to help him endure the hardships of almost thirty years in prison, the deaths of loved ones, the limited contact with family and friends. Nelson Mandela was known for his disciplined approach to life and for fighting for justice, even in Robben Island Prison he continued to fight for his rights and the rights of other inmates.

- "Isolation and being deprived of certain diet, certain meals...rice water, that's all. Sometimes when the sentence is long, you fast. I'm not sure now whether it's for two days , and then you have a break, you eat, and the next you continue fasting and then on the fifth day, they give you food again. Stengel: How did you deal with the hunger? Mandela:...The human body has got enormous capacity for adjusting, especially if...you can coordinate your thinking, your whole spiritual approach to the physical one. And if you are convinced that you are doing something right, that you are demonstrating to the authorities that you can defend your rights and fight back, you don't feel it all." (Mandela, 2010, p.144)

- "And you found you know, the resistance, the ability of the human spirit to resist injustice right inside prison. And...you learn that you don't have to have a degree to have the qualities of leader, the qualities of a man who wants to fight injustice wherever he is..." (Mandela, 2010, p.254)

- While visiting the Nelson Mandela exhibit (July 16th, 2021) at the Milwaukee Public Museum I observed one of the prayer journals that Mandela kept while in Robben Island Prison. It was clear to me the power of prayer sustained Mandela and empowered him to keep fighting against injustice of apartheid and racism for South Africa and for himself and other prisoners at Robben Island. (Nelson Mandela Exhibit, 2021)

Nelson Mandela was known for his gracious humility; would help in whatever way he could and he knew the freedom movement was not about him.

- "...I had no problem, you see, in cleaning the bucket of another. And it was just to help a friend..."To know that you are the object of such goodwill makes one humble indeed. And that is how I felt." (Mandela, 2010, p.149)

- Mandela understood that good men and women worldwide stood for peace and that their efforts and achievements would be remembered even when they passed away, that their legacy would live forever. (Mandela, 2010, p.409)

- Nelson Mandela often said, "I'm not a saint, unless you think of a saint as a sinner who keeps on trying." (Pillay, 2013)

Mandela relied on his prayer life, the prayers of others and drew inspiration from other political leaders fighting for justice, especially from Martin Luther King Jr. In the book "In the Spiritual Mandela - Faith and Religion in the Life of Nelson Mandel by Dennis Cruywagen,

- MLK Jr's Letter from Birmingham Jail had a profound impact on Mandela that the "letter will stay with me for years, saying as it does that the key to overcoming injustice and becoming a tool for reconciliation is to summon up the faith and courage to overcome inaction and fear in the face of division and suspicion." MLK Jr's Letter from Birmingham Jail had a profound impact on Mandela that stayed with him for many years.

- "According to Wiggett, Mandela's spirituality was a significant reason for the steadfastness and courage he showed throughout his life. Mandela's faith and trust in God guided him through the difficult times and helped him to cope with the pain of his imprisonment." "This is why, "Wiggett explains, "when he went in, he was one thing; when he came out he was ripe, spiritually strong and he was whole." (Cruywagen, 2018, p.120-121)

- "...Mandela therefore saw it as his duty to personally stand up for the beliefs of every person it was required to protect. This is why he chose to keep matters relating to his faith private, even if it had been crucial in alleviating many of his anxieties and fears during the long year of his incarceration, and through all the challenges of his presidency." (Cruywagen, 2018, p.XX)

- Mandela said, "We appeal to you all to pray and work for peace. The violence must be ended and those who fuel it must be brought to justice. We cannot afford to fail! For success we ask you all to remember us in your prayers." (Mandela, 2010, p. 417)

- "...he(Mandela) said to her (Brigalia Bam): "This is a very important day in our lives. It's an important day, but we trust you as a woman of prayer." "That showed that he based his trust on whether the election would be free of violence on the faith of those who were organizing it. Here someone (Mandela) who perceived faith and prayer as vital components for bringing success and unity to the election." (Cruywagen, 2018, p.136)

- "...Vearey discovered just how much Mandela depended on his faith to guide him through the trials he faced every day. Vearey remembers one occasion, at a hotel in Cape Town in 1993, when he entered Mandela's room one morning to find the politician praying with a Bible next to him." "Vearey came to realize that this was typical of Mandela's morning routine: he would pray and study the Bible (which he also read every night, Vearey says)." (Cruywagen, 2018, p.130)

Nelson Mandela could see religious manipulators' use of God's name to oppress the poor. He remained committed to the liberation of all oppressed people in South Africa.

- "The moral decay of some communities in various parts of the world reveals itself among others in the use of the name of God to justify the maintenance of actions which are condemned by the entire world as crimes against humanity." (Mandela, 2010, p. 403)

- "Among the multitude of those who have throughout history committed themselves to the struggle for justice in all its implications, are some of those who have commanded invincible liberation armies who waged stirring operations and sacrificed enormously in order to free their people from the yoke of oppression, to better their lives by creating jobs, building houses, schools, hospitals, introducing electricity, and bringing clean and healthy water to people especially in the rural areas. Their aim was to remove the gap between the rich and the poor, the educated and the uneducated, the healthy and those afflicted by preventable diseases."
(Mandela, 2010, p.403)

- Vukile Mehana says, "Mandela promoted reconciliation and forgiveness because he considered it to be his duty – a duty that was bestowed on him by God. The empathy Mandela shared with those who had suffered past wrongs, and with the poor and displaced, informed his leadership of the country. As a servant of God, he fervently believed that he existed to serve these people." (Cruywagen, 2018, p.169)

- In the internet article, "Mandela and the confession of a closet Christian" by Verashni Pillay Mandela's faith and prayer life are revealed. "Nelson Mandela was apparently a man of great faith, who kept his Christian beliefs discreet in favour of his great life work of reconciliation. That is the picture emerging from a number of ministers who regularly met to pray with Mandela in prison as well as throughout part of his life."
"He was a deeply religious man; he believed sincerely in the existence of the Almighty," said Bishop Don Dabula, who first met Mandela in 1962 and met to pray with him whenever he was his home in Qunu.

Mandela's exhibited great faith and even greater capacity to forgive and reconcile. One has to ask themself how is that possible without divine intervention through prayer? In spite of being told that he would never be released from prison by different Prime Ministers, attorneys and wardens.

- In the book, "A Real-Life Story Nelson Mandela South African Revolutionary","Mandela refused to believe, in spite of their life sentences, that he and his friends would die in prison."

- Mandela's capacity to forgive was enormous! Mandela put it this way: "Hating clouds the mind, he pointed out. It gets in the way of strategy. Leaders cannot afford to hate."

- Not only did he forgive greatly, but he had an amazing capacity to reconcile with others and encourage blacks and whites to do the same. "Instead he bent all his efforts to bind the country together and heal the deep wounds of apartheid."

- Mandela also in Time Magazine, "Nelson Mandela A Hero's Journey, "A year after taking office, he collaborated with the respected Archbishop Desmond Tutu to establish the Truth and Reconciliation Commission...charged with investigating the human-rights abuses of the apartheid era, the commission had the power to grant amnesty to those who confessed."

- "Through this body (TRC), Mandela succeeded in making the willingness of each side to offer and accept forgiveness something close to a patriotic duty and helped heal his land." (Knauer, 2013, p.113)

Nelson Mandela was the first elected black President of South Africa, ended the apartheid movement, brought healing to South Africa, won the Nobel Peace Prize and so many other prestigious awards. Prayer was an essential part of his life; it helped to shape and transform him from the armed struggle to the non-violent movement.

In the book, "Faith & Courage Praying With Mandela", "For the last eleven weeks of his life, Nelson Mandela and his family were soaked in prayer by people at home and abroad." "Bishop Malusi Mpumlwana was long-time friend of Mandela and was saying Mandela's favourite blessing prayer as he passed away on December 5th, 2013:

> Numbers 6:24-26 "May the Lord bless you and keep you. May the Lord make his face to shine upon you and be gracious to you. May the Lord look upon you with kindness, and give you peace." (Cruywagen, 2018, p.180)

Desmond Tutu

As I researched Bishop Desmond Tutu, I was delighted to find out that he was a man of prayer, committed to praying early in the morning, noon, evening, and throughout the day. He even had prayer companions that would pray for him daily. The spiritual responsibilities he faced would have been too hard to continue without a solid prayer life. Bishop Tutu cherished being a pastor and having genuine interactions with his church members. He saw the horrors of apartheid and wanted to do all that he could to treat everyone, especially black South Africans with dignity. "He had the compassion of his mother, becoming an emotional, caring pastor who intuitively felt the plight of the weak and burned with outrage at abuses of power by the strong." (Allen, 2006, p.145)

Desmond Tutu knew at an early age that God would use him mightily, similarly the way Mother Teresa knew at a young age too. Yet it was clear for Tutu that he had such loving examples that he could not just pray or just spring into action only. Therefore, Tutu carried out the true mandates of the true church of Jesus Christ with passion, boldness and relentlessness. "The example set by the Community of Resurrection, which taught him that the choice was not either prayer or social action: rather, prayer inevitably drove you off your knees into action." (Allen, 2006, p.395) Michael Battle stated, "Tutu's life invites all of us to never detach the spiritual life from our real life. Our prayers must be real and tactile, and move us to action." Tutu stated, "We are involved with God to set us free from all that enslaves us and makes us less than what He intended us to be." (Battle, 2021, p.312)

Bishop Desmond Tutu saw the value and power of prayer and action, he was known for having prayer vigils and then going out to march when God told him to, despite the pushback that they hadn't notified enough leaders yet.

- "..He organized at the cathedral a twenty-four-hour prayer vigil for racial harmony, at which special prayer were said for people detained without trial under the Terrorism Act." (Allen, 2006, p.150)

- "In June 1976 the South African youths had, had enough and were rioting. "On June 17, Tutu called for twenty-four hours of prayer and fasting for the "miracle of a change of heart" by the government."

- "In May of 1980, when a fellow minister, John Thorne was detained by police, his colleagues met and agreed that if he was not released, they would gather at the church's head office on Monday morning; hold a prayer service for him; and in defiance of a law prohibiting public protest, walk to John Vorster Square to hand in a petition for his release." (Allen, 2006, p.185)

- The clergy were arrested and detained themselves. "In their cells, the men prayed, sang hymns, and told stories and jokes." "During a prayer service before the hearing, Joe Wing wept: in his time in the ecumenical movement, he had never seen denominational differences evaporate as they did then."

- "..Tutu led a week of prayer and fasting against forced removals..." Bishop Tutu knew that he could not ignore the oppression (poverty, violence, & hatred of apartheid). (Allen, 2006, p.201)

- "Tutu would say after praying, "We will march tomorrow." He did not consult anyone even church leaders, "because he simply knew what God was calling him to do."" (Battle, 2021, p.41)

- "Tutu made his mark when he arrived at the SACC by introducing compulsory daily staff prayers; regular Bible study; monthly Eucharist; and silent retreats."

- "So for us prayer, meditations, Bible reading are not peripheral to our operations. These things are at the center of our lives. We are not embarrassed that we put God first...Our pattern and example is our Lord and Savior Jesus Christ who could be the man for others only because he was first and foremost a man of God, a man of prayer."

For Desmond Tutu prayer and action went hand in hand like a well fit glove on one's hand. Not only did Tutu participate in protests he had a GOD to obey and answer too, therefore he was COMPELLED TO SPEAK OUT.

- "We give thanks for Steve (Biko) and for his life and his death…Steve started something that is quite unstoppable. The powers of injustice, of oppression, of exploitation, have done their worst and they have lost. They have lost because they are immoral and wrong and our God, the God of the Exodus, the liberator God, is a God of justice and liberation and goodness. Our cause, the cause of justice and liberation, must triumph because it' is moral and just and right." (Allen, 2006, p.164)

- "..So we say to the perpetrators of racism and apartheid, your policies are immoral, are unchristian, are unbiblical. You are taking on God for you are saying, God has made a mistake, that God, when he created some black, has made a ghastly mistake that they have to go around apologizing for their existence. We don't have to apologize for our existence! God created us in his own image." (Battle, 2021, p.166)

- "Moses went to Pharoah repeatedly to secure the release of the Israelites. The prophets spoke repeatedly to the kings and too the people to get them to change and learn to obey God. We too as churches will go on speaking to the government until the very last moment." (Allen, 2006, p.188)

- "But he (Tutu) said that, like the Old Testament prophet Jeremiah, he had no choice but to speak his mind. If Jeremiah tried to suppress God's word, it became imprisoned within him like "a fire burning in his breast." When God's children hurt, said Tutu, he too could not keep quiet." (Allen, 2006, p.221)

- "But God told me and I'm afraid we can't argue with God…." "It looks as if I'm arrogant and presumptuous, yes, but the trouble is that I knew I was not my own master. At least I believed that." (Allen, 2006, p.308)

- Tutu encouraged the church to sign the Free Mandela petition. "Soon Tutu was telling the BBC's southern African correspondent, John Humphrys that Mandela would be prime minister within five to ten years."

Tutu's humility was observed and appreciated by many.

- Frank Ferrari commented, "There was never a conflict between the man and the politician – he was first and foremost the priest against social injustice and oppression….When he walked into a room….the humility and commitment and dedication of this person that struck everyone [and] his irrepressible personality with his magnificent sense of humor." (Allen, 2006, p.241)

- In Desmond Tutu A Spiritual Biography, When Tutu visited the Home for Derelicts in Calcutta he, "experienced then divine love incarnate in the ministrations of those nuns, who treated their charges with a deep reverence as if they were caring for Jesus Christ."

- Tutu knew his mantle (the baton) would be passed on to other leaders to continue to fight for justice. He was known for mentoring, training and promoting women; he was not confined to patriarchal stereotypes.

- Tutu humbly admitted that God and his prayer life gave him strength to endure all the opposition and the terrible experiences of apartheid.

Bishop Tutu had enemies nevertheless he had greater faith in God and prayed for his enemies,

- "Tutu had the strength, the conviction, and the commitment to do what God called him to do. This was also courageous, since Tutu was on numerous death lists and certainly could have been assassinated by the clandestine security police. Nevertheless, Tutu was convinced that God would protect him." (Battle, 2021, p.41)

- "But whites' anger against him was first exposed in obscene phone calls and death threats from the far right."

- "…Paul Erasmus and about ten other security policemen…discussed stabbing Tutu with a sharpened bicycle spoke." "In the late 1990s, a white former military officer seconded to Venda told Storey and Tutu that he had ordered them killed and still did not know why his orders had not been carried out."

- Amazingly Tutu saw the damage that apartheid did to both blacks and whites. "He had thought he was coming back to South Africa to reassure blacks that God loved them and they should assert themselves; he found that "in many ways it was whites who needed to hear this message about self-assurance and self-acceptance, that oppression dehumanized the oppressor as much as if not more than, the oppressed."

- "Whether I like it or not, whether he likes it or not…P.W. Botha is my brother and I must desire and pray for the best for him." (Allen, 2006, p.266-267)

Tutu's prayer life was essential to him and could not survive without it. He shared his prayer ministry with others and was known to be a man of prayer.

- "Tutu stated, "I know, for myself, that I could not survive at all, if I did not worship, if I did not meditate, if I did not try to have those moments of quiet to be with the Lord. I would not be able to survive. I would collapse." (Battle, 2021, p.152)

- "It soon became apparent to the staff at Bishopcourt that Tutu the ebullient extrovert and Tutu the meditative priest who needed six or seven hours a day in silence were two sides of the same coin." (Allen, 2006, p.275)

- It was even known that Tutu was able to respond with such love and care because of his disciplined prayer life.

- "He developed a ministry of prayer on the telephone (which was extended to heads of state such as Nelson Mandela, and later to Bill Clinton in the White House)"

- It's interesting that even when Bishop Tutu had angered enemies and allies someone would step in with a rebuttal that credited the call of God on his life. "He is a man of deep prayer and living faith and spends more time on his knees (in prayer) than most of those who call for action to be taken by the Church against him." (Allen, 2006, p.179)

- "..having heard Bishop Tutu's reasons for his statement, we share his belief that any retraction of or apology for his statement in this instance would constitute a denial of his prophetic calling...We will not allow any single member of the Body of Christ to be isolated for attack."

- Bishop Tutu had been complimented by Timothy Bavin, "One man has-by God's grace – done more for the cause of justice, peace and reconciliation in this Diocese and City than many of us have achieve in many years...and that in less than a year."

- "(Senator) Kennedy's senior aide Gregory Craig, "The reason he was important was that whenever we saw him, he was acting courageously and consistently with his nonviolent position and his spiritual leadership position. He was the closest thing to a Dr. King the antiapartheid movement had." (Allen, 2006, p.262)

- In fact Michael Battle wrote this biography because of "Tutu's intense spirituality embodies his relentless fight against apartheid."

Tutu had a gift to see how apartheid was truly racism and even the labels that the oppressor tried to use to justify the horrific realities of hatred, oppression and poverty:

- "Tutu astutely observed that despite the obnoxious label given to South African violence by the media, black-on-black violence, "I have never heard them describe Bosnia or Northern Ireland as the scene of white on white violence." (Battle, 2021, p.116)

- Bishop Tutu stood up against apartheid indifferent ways, "Tutu told a London correspondent of South African newspaper group that he would refuse to apply for government permission to live in the dean's official resident in the white suburb of Houghton."

- Tutu knew that God's law was higher than man's law. "And unfortunately too many have been brainwashed into thinking that legally right and morally right mean the same thing." (Battle, 2021, p.193)

- "Tutu was more specific, as he believed that Jesus Christ called all people to freedom- not just some. Jesus' gospel (good news to the poor) demands that we struggle for justice and peace, compassion and reconciliation, for laughter, joy, and life, which belong to the kingdom of God." (Battle, 2021, p.68)

- Barney Pityana can recall protesting as a student that Desmond was the only one who stepped in between himself other students and the police, dogs and tear gas. In Rabble Rouser for Peace, "Desmond [came] almost from nowhere, in a cassock...broke the police cordon and came to be among us. I recall moving scenes of young women kneeling to pray with Desmond for blessings. Even today when I recall that I get very emotional. For me that was the greatest example I could think, of what to be a priest was about."

- It was when the South African government moved to arrest, detain, exile and kill the political activists is when the church leaders and church picked up where they left off. In 1968 "A Message to the People of South Africa" where it was clear that apartheid was against the true gospel of Jesus Christ and what the GOD of the Bible stood for. "This doctrine of separation is a false faith, a novel gospel."

- (Desmond Tutu A Spiritual Biography) "We see how Tutu's identity was formed by his courageous struggle against the violence of racial categorization. South African leaders like Tutu risked their lives in order to envision a whole South African in which not only black and white people co-existed, but all people."

Tutu had expectations of who Christians should be like and what they should do. But most importantly he role modeled the expectation until he passed away on December 26th, 2021. "We expect them to reflect the character of Jesus Christ. We expect Christians to be gentle, not always quarrelling and scratching. We expect Christians to be humble as Jesus was humble...We expect Christians to be peace-loving and people who work for peace. We expect Christians to be loving...We expect Christians to be people who forgive as Jesus forgave even those who were nailing him to the Cross. But we expect Christians also to be those who stand up for the truth, we expect Christians to be those who stand up for justice, we expect Christians to be those who stand on the side of the poor and the hungry and the homeless and the naked, and when that happens then Christians will be trustworthy, believable witnesses." (Battle, 2021)

Please note that if a page number is missing or incorrect from a source that it is not intentional. I pray for grace and understanding for any mistakes made in the thesis.

Chapter 5 - Conclusion
Results

The Six Great Names were tested by The Prayer Empowerment Theory four core questionnaires

1) Appendix A - The Six Great Names Prayer Empowerment Questionnaire

   1. Did she or he pray first?
   2. Did God guide her or his fight against injustice?
   3. Did she or he obey God?
   4. Did she or he have a heart for the "Least of These"?
   5. Did she or he endure afflictions?
   6. Did she or he continue to pray?
   7. Did she or he sacrifice to improve the lives of others?
   8. Did she or he achieve what was said to be impossible?
   9. Did she or he leave a legacy?

2) Appendix B - The Six Great Names Prayer Foundation Questionnaire

   1. Did she or he pray first?
   2. Did she or he pray daily?
   3. Did she or he pray throughout the day?
   4. Did she or he ask God for help?
   5. Did she or he value their prayer life?
   6. Did she or he see prayer as a foundation to justice?
   7. Did she or he use prayer and action to fight for justice?
   8. Did she or he have faith in Jesus Christ?
   9. Did she or he view Jesus Christ as a role model?

3) Appendix C - The Six Great Names Fight For Justice Questionnaire

   1. Did God direct she or he?
   2. Did she or he know what injustice was?
   3. Did she or he know what justice was?
   4. Did she or he care for the "Least of These"?
   5. Did she or he face great adversity?
   6. Did she or he know God's calling?
   7. Did she or he pay a cost to fight for justice?
   8. Is she or he considered an Activist?
   9. Has she or he made a difference?

4) Appendix D - The Six Great Names Prayer Outcome Questionnaire

   1. Did she or he ask God for help?
   2. Did God send she or he help?
   3. Did she or he ask God for strength?
   4. Did she or he ask God for courage?
   5. Did she or he ask God for insights?
   6. Did she or he endure and overcome?
   7. Did she or he receive awards/honors?
   8. Did she or he achieve greater works?
   9. Did she or he leave a legacy?

The answer was Yes for all the Six Great Names in all the questionnaires. That was a total of 36 questions all Yes or 36 Questions at 6 out of 6 at 100%.

Summary

In summary the six great names, Ruby Bridges, Mother Teresa, Coretta Scott King, Martin Luther King Jr., Nelson Mandela, and Desmond Tutu all: (See Chapter 3 – The Prayer Empowerment Theory & Appendices A-D)

- Prayed to Jesus Christ and Father God, their faith was a Christian (Kingdom) faith.

- Prayed daily, the exact hours are not exactly known for each one, but they did not go a day without praying.

- Faced God-sized Callings, Tasks, Afflictions, Fears and Opposition that only God could empower them to endure and overcome.

- Empowered by God to start, continue and finish their God Ordained Destiny

- Achieved what was deemed impossible: end racial segregation, begin racial integration, gain equal rights, provide and protect the poor, numerous prestigious awards, etc.

- People were aware of their prayer lives, admired them for it and learned from their example.

- Observed all of them considered prayer as a way of life, were thankful to be partners with God Almighty and Jesus Christ, they surrendered totally to God.

- Viewed justice as all were created equal by Father God, therefore all should be treated with dignity, love, respect and equity through education, economics, healthcare, religion, employment, nutrition, housing, safety, etc.

- Knew it was sinful and shameful to "highjack the faith" to oppress and degrade anyone deemed inferior. World peace cannot exist with oppression, poverty, and violence.

- Drew strength from their prayer lives, the prayers of others, Holy scriptures, the sufferings of the Least of These.

- Admired Jesus Christ's example of prayer, long-suffering, forgiveness, and endurance. (To some extent each admired one another.)

- Fought for justice because God called them to it, they didn't give up and obeyed God.

- Empowered prayer kept them going

- Used prayer to empower them into committed action.

- See Appendix S – Accomplishments vs Afflictions

- Faced death threats, verbal assaults, overwhelming pressures, their own fears, etc.

GOD calls ordinary people to do extraordinary things. As I studied them, I noticed what they all had in common: (See Appendices F-S)

1. Faithful Prayer Life
2. A willingness to OBEY GOD
3. A Heart for the Least of These
4. Surrendering One's Life/Major Sacrifices
5. Courage to Continue, Overcome & FINISH
6. A refusal to give up!
7. A Desire, Loving Ability to Pray and Forgive One's Enemies
8. A gift to MOTIVATE OTHERS
9. HUMILITY

The six GREAT Names – Martin Luther King Jr, Coretta Scott King, Mother Teresa, Nelson Mandela, Desmond Tutu, and Ruby Bridges all fully embodied the Prayer Empowerment Theory four Core Outlines: The Prayer Empowerment Theory Outline, The Prayer Foundation Outline, The Fight for Justice Outline and The Prayer Outcome Outline. (See Appendices A-D, F & G)

The Prayer Empowerment Theory Outline:

1. She or he prayed first, (usually a silent Jesus Christ Centered Prayer)
2. God spoke to them on what they were to do for Him in the fight for justice.
3. She or he obeyed God wholeheartedly.
4. Had a heart for the "least of these".
5. Endured intense hardships, afflictions.
6. Continued their prayer life.
7. Sacrificed so others could live a better life.
8. Achieved what was deemed IMPOSSIBLE.
9. Left a legacy that still inspires and lives on to this day.

The Prayer Foundation Outline:

1. She or he prayed first.
2. She or he prayed daily.
3. Prayed throughout the day.
4. She or he asked God for help.
5. She or he valued their prayer life.
6. Saw prayer as a foundation to justice.
7. Used prayer and action to fight for justice.
8. She or he had faith (kept faith) in Jesus Christ.
9. She or he stated (viewed) Jesus Christ as a key role model.

The Fight for Justice Outline:

1. God directed she or he (through prayer).
2. She or he knew what injustice was.
3. She or he knew what justice was.
4. She or he cared for the "least of these".
5. She or he faced great adversity.
6. She or he knew God's calling.
7. There was a cost to fight for justice.
8. She or he is considered an Activist.
9. She or he made a difference.

The Prayer Outcome Outline:

1. She or he asked God for help.
2. God sent help.
3. She or he asked God for strength.
4. She or he asked God for courage.
5. She or he asked God for insights.
6. She or he endured and overcame.
7. She or he received award/honors.
8. She or he achieved greater works.
9. She or he left a (lasting) legacy.

All six Great Names lived out each of the Prayer Empowerment Theory Concept Maps, which are all interconnected (in the Appendices F-Q): Prayer Empowerment Theory, Prayer Transformation, Acknowledges God, "Least of These", Identify Injustice, Fighting Injustice, Dealing With Tragedy, Obedience, Miracles-Signs-

Wonders, Pass the Baton, Great Follower to Great Leader and Path to Greatness. The four questionnaires used to test the Prayer Empowerment Theory are reflected in the Prayer Empowerment Theory Concept Maps.

Conclusion

As I analyzed the prayer lives of Ruby Bridges, Mother Teresa, Coretta Scott King, Martin Luther King Jr., Nelson Mandela and Desmond Tutu through the lens of The Prayer Empowerment Theory I learned that their prayer lives gave them the strength to do great exploits for Almighty God. I observed that each had a great deal of humility to depend on God, to pray for their enemies and to forgive their enemies too. Even when they were villainized, suffered great tragedies, afflictions they continued to pray and chose love over hate. Their uncanny ability to endure the Garden of Gethsemane moments, carry their crosses to keep fighting for justice for the "Least of These" with a true servant's heart, they chose to be better and not bitter could not be done without their faithful prayer lives.

They were all familiar with the various types of prayer: petitioning prayer, empowerment prayer, adoration prayer, forgiveness prayer, intercessory prayer, lamenting prayer, serenity prayer, Silent Jesus Christ Centered prayer, successor prayer, and thanksgiving prayer which is evident in their quality and extensive prayer life with Jesus Christ.

The six Great Names of Justice all viewed Jesus Christ as their role model. They embraced how Jesus Christ prayed often and withdrew to secluded places to pray and be alone with Father God, Luke 5:15-16. They followed in Jesus Christ's footsteps and were not chasing fame or seeking greatness. They were all about their Father in Heaven's business and He rewarded them with divine destiny helpers, miracles, signs & wonders, and a divine greatness that no one can take away from them. (See Appendices Q – Path to Greatness Map and S – Accomplishments vs Afflictions)

Each of the six Great Names acknowledged God for answering their prayers of sent resources, help and Godly stewardship abilities. All of the six Great Names had been through their Wilderness Preparation & Testing and Prayer Transformation that called them higher to do greater works for God's glory. That Luke 14:11 manifested in the six Great Names because of their humility and divine collaboration/partnership with Father God they were able to birth out their God Sized Calling through continued empowered prayer to fulfill their God Given Destiny. Their humility shined forth in how they gladly passed the baton, without resentment because the work they did was a part of a higher calling, and it could not die with them.

The six Great Names of Justice embraced the two-way street of prayer, not the one-way street. It was important that they spent time with God early before the start of the day so they could get their instructions on what God required of them for that day. They all new from an early age that God had something great for them to do whether through prayer, an inner knowing/feeling or through dreams or visions from Almighty God. Through righteous indignation they had an amazing ability to identify injustice as hijacking of the faith, religious manipulators, oppressors/goliaths, poverty, violence, police brutality, discrimination, segregation, etc. The Great knew when poverty, violence, chaos, hatred, oppression, etc. were present, that meant justice was absent. Not only did they draw the line between right and wrong, justice and injustice, through empowered prayer...THEY STOOD UP FOR JUSTICE.

On November 3, 2014 Ruby Bridges said to an audience, "Somebody has to have courage enough to stand up, to make a change." (Bridges, Ruby Bridges and The Problem We All (Still) Live With, Internet Blog) **Are you that courageous somebody who must stand up and fight for justice?**

Ecuador's Attorney General in 2024 is Diana Salazar Mendez, and she has made Time Magazine's "The 100 Most Influential People of 2024". Mendez is fighting for justice in Ecuador and like Jesus Christ and the Great Names has received death threats, harassment, but she's not letting that stop her. Mendez says it best that, "It's time to tell all of Ecuador that justice will not kneel down." (Power, Times Magazine, April 17, 2024) I second her stance that, **It's time to tell all of the world that justice will not kneel down.**

In closing the power of prayer works because those people we view as great humbled themselves and realized that what GOD was calling them to do there is no way they could do it in their own strength. They knew they could not start, continue, or finish without GOD's continual help. (See Appendix F - Prayer Empowerment Theory Map) When GOD called them, He never promised them that it would be easy and without struggles. GOD would always be there because they prayed, even when it seemed He had abandoned them.

Through empowered prayer, faith, dedication, and discipline I could write, research, test and provide quality and substantial evidence that before they were known as great names they prayed first. That prayer is the foundation to justice in not just the six great names I researched but many others as well.

Appendix A – The Prayer Empowerment Questionnaire

Appendix A – The Six Great Names Prayer Empowerment Questionnaire

Six Great Names Prayer Empowerment Theory Questionnaire

Directions: Please answer with a Yes or No in the box.

	Mother Teresa	Ruby Bridges	Coretta Scott King	MLK Jr	Nelson Mandela	Desmond Tutu
1. Did she or he pray first?	Yes	Yes	Yes	Yes	Yes	Yes
2. Did God direct (speak or lead) them in their fight against injustice?	Yes	Yes	Yes	Yes	Yes	Yes
3. Did she or he obey God?	Yes	Yes	Yes	Yes	Yes	Yes
4. Did she or he have a heart for the "Least of These"?	Yes	Yes	Yes	Yes	Yes	Yes
5. Did she or he endure afflictions?	Yes	Yes	Yes	Yes	Yes	Yes
6. Did she or he continue to pray?	Yes	Yes	Yes	Yes	Yes	Yes
7. Did she or he Sacrifice to improve others' lives?	Yes	Yes	Yes	Yes	Yes	Yes
8. Achieve the impossible?	Yes	Yes	Yes	Yes	Yes	Yes
9. Did she or he leave a legacy?	Yes	Yes	Yes	Yes	Yes	Yes

Six Great Names Prayer Empowerment Theory Questionnaire Results

1. Did she or he pray first?	6 out of 6	100%
2. Did God guide their fight against injustice?	6 out of 6	100%
3. Did she or he obey God?	6 out of 6	100%
4. Have a heart for the "Least of These"?	6 out of 6	100%
5. Did she or he endure afflictions?	6 out of 6	100%
6. Did she or he continue to pray?	6 out of 6	100%
7. Sacrifice to improve the lives of others?	6 out of 6	100%
8. Achieve what was said to be impossible?	6 out of 6	100%
9. Did she or he leave a legacy?	6 out of 6	100%

Appendix B – The Prayer Foundation Questionnaire

Appendix B – The Six Great Names Prayer Foundation Questionnaire

Six Great Names Prayer Foundation Questionnaire

Directions: Please answer with a Yes or No in the box.

	Mother Teresa	Ruby Bridges	Coretta Scott King	MLK Jr	Nelson Mandela	Desmond Tutu
1. Did she or he pray first?	Yes	Yes	Yes	Yes	Yes	Yes
2. Did she or he pray daily?	Yes	Yes	Yes	Yes	Yes	Yes
3. Pray throughout the day?	Yes	Yes	Yes	Yes	Yes	Yes
4. Did she or he ask God for help?	Yes	Yes	Yes	Yes	Yes	Yes
5. Did she or he value their prayer life?	Yes	Yes	Yes	Yes	Yes	Yes
6. See prayer as a foundation to justice?	Yes	Yes	Yes	Yes	Yes	Yes
7. Use prayer and action to fight for justice?	Yes	Yes	Yes	Yes	Yes	Yes
8. Have faith in Jesus Christ?	Yes	Yes	Yes	Yes	Yes	Yes
9. Was Jesus Christ the role model?	Yes	Yes	Yes	Yes	Yes	Yes

Six Great Names Prayer Foundation Questionnaire Results

1. Did she or he pray first?	6 out of 6	100%
2. Did she or he pray daily?	6 out of 6	100%
3. Pray throughout the day?	6 out of 6	100%
4. Did she or he ask God for help?	6 out of 6	100%
5. Did she or he value their prayer life?	6 out of 6	100%
6. See prayer as foundation to justice?	6 out of 6	100%
7. Use prayer and action to fight for justice?	6 out of 6	100%
8. Have faith in Jesus Christ?	6 out of 6	100%
9. Was Jesus Christ the role model?	6 out of 6	100%

Appendix C – The Fight for Justice Questionnaire

Appendix C – The Six Great Names Fight for Justice Questionnaire

Six Great Names Fight for Justice Questionnaire

Directions: Please answer with a Yes or No in the box.

	Mother Teresa	Ruby Bridges	Coretta Scott King	MLK Jr	Nelson Mandela	Desmond Tutu
1. Did God direct she or he?	Yes	Yes	Yes	Yes	Yes	Yes
2. Know what injustice was?	Yes	Yes	Yes	Yes	Yes	Yes
3. Know what justice was?	Yes	Yes	Yes	Yes	Yes	Yes
4. Did she or he care for "L.o.T."?	Yes	Yes	Yes	Yes	Yes	Yes
5. Did she or he face great adversity?	Yes	Yes	Yes	Yes	Yes	Yes
6. Did she or he know God's calling?	Yes	Yes	Yes	Yes	Yes	Yes
7. Was there a cost to fight for justice?	Yes	Yes	Yes	Yes	Yes	Yes
8. Is she or he considered an Activist?	Yes	Yes	Yes	Yes	Yes	Yes
9. Has she or he made a difference?	Yes	Yes	Yes	Yes	Yes	Yes

Six Great Names Fight for Justice Questionnaire Results

1. Did God direct she or he to fight for justice?	6 out of 6	100%
2. Did she or he know what injustice was?	6 out of 6	100%
3. Did she or he know what justice was?	6 out of 6	100%
4. Did she or he care for the "Least of These" (L.O.T.)?	6 out of 6	100%
5. Did she or he face great adversity?	6 out of 6	100%
6. Did she or he know God's calling?	6 out of 6	100%
7. Was there a cost to fight for justice?	6 out of 6	100%
8. Is she or he considered an Activist?	6 out of 6	100%
9. Has she or he made a (historical) difference?	6 out of 6	100%

*L.o.T = Least of These

Appendix D – The Prayer Outcome Questionnaire

Appendix D – The Six Great Names Prayer Outcome Questionnaire

Six Great Names Prayer Outcome Questionnaire

Directions: Please answer with a Yes or No in the box.

	Mother Teresa	Ruby Bridges	Coretta Scott King	MLK Jr	Nelson Mandela	Desmond Tutu
1. Did she or he ask God for help?	Yes	Yes	Yes	Yes	Yes	Yes
2. Did God send help?	Yes	Yes	Yes	Yes	Yes	Yes
3. Did she or he ask God for strength?	Yes	Yes	Yes	Yes	Yes	Yes
4. Did she or he ask God for courage?	Yes	Yes	Yes	Yes	Yes	Yes
5. Did she or he ask God for insights?	Yes	Yes	Yes	Yes	Yes	Yes
6. Did she or he endure and overcome?	Yes	Yes	Yes	Yes	Yes	Yes
7. Did she or he receive award/honors?	Yes	Yes	Yes	Yes	Yes	Yes
8. Did she or he achieve greater works?	Yes	Yes	Yes	Yes	Yes	Yes
9. Did she or he leave a legacy?	Yes	Yes	Yes	Yes	Yes	Yes

Six Great Names Prayer Outcome Questionnaire Results

1. Did she or he ask God for help?	6 out of 6	100%
2. Did God send help?	6 out of 6	100%
3. Did she or he ask God for strength?	6 out of 6	100%
4. Did she or he ask God for courage?	6 out of 6	100%
5. Did she or he ask God for insights?	6 out of 6	100%
6. Did she or he endure and overcome?	6 out of 6	100%
7. Did she or he receive award/honors?	6 out of 6	100%
8. Did she or he achieve greater works?	6 out of 6	100%
9. Did she or he leave a legacy?	6 out of 6	100%

Appendix E - Glossary

Acknowledges God = Consistently gives credit and glory to God for accomplishments, helping, leading/directing, comforting them, answering prayers, etc.

Action = When one is empowered through prayer to stand up for justice, to help the least of these and make a lasting difference in their lives, understanding faith without works is dead. James 2:17

Affliction = Suffering various hardships, disappointments, betrayals, sabotages, hinderances, interferences, opposing forces, etc.

"Birthing Out" = God has blessed each person with a calling, assignments, destiny – yet it must be prayed out through seeking God and following His instructions to bring them into existence, to complete the calling, the assignment and fulfill one's God Given Destiny.

Called to Carry One's Cross = Although difficult one understands no cross, no crown. One must endure hardships of varying levels, while partnering with GOD, to role model how to carry one's cross (suffering/afflictions) while still serving God and humanity especially in the fight for justice. Mark 8:34

Collaborators/Partners = Matured to a higher prayer life and Christ Spiritual Maturity to surrender (Asked God what they can do for Him?).

Disciples (of Christ) = Followers of Jesus Christ's teachings, lifestyle and commandments. They have surrendered their life for Jesus Christ's mission, and God's perfected will for their lives. They are known as **Kingdom Believers**.

Divine Destiny Helpers = When one prays for help, God sends people who are assigned to help the leader (praying, working, fundraising, volunteering, recruiting, etc.) His will concerning fighting for justice (helping the poor, the least of these, etc.) and other means of advancing the Kingdom of God.

Divine Greatness = When God shines His light on specific people who partner with Him in prayer, obedience, humility to accomplish a God Sized Calling and live out a God Given Destiny. These people are remembered and make their mark on history.

Doer of God's Word = When one obeys God's Holy Bible (scriptures) to the best of their ability, obeys God's specific instructions for one's life and lives a consistent Godly lifestyle. James 1:21-27

Faith = A strong belief, trust and dependency on Jesus Christ, the Holy Spirit, Almighty God, His instructions, prophecies, and the Holy Bible, that brings about salvation, deliverance, healing, provision, comfort, miracles, signs, and wonders.

Faithful = When one is consistently devoted to the Kingdom of God through prayer, a "Doer" of God's word lifestyle (lives what one preaches, teaches and prays) and a Godly role model to others.

Foundation = A symbolic bedrock of a starting point or a main ingredient (prayer) that the Great Names of Justice used to fight for justice and advance the Kingdom of God here on earth by praying in Jesus Christ Name. Matthew 7:24-25, 1 Corinthians 3:10-11, John 14:12-14

Garden of Gethsemane Prayer (Moment) = When Jesus wrestled with the agony of being crucified, yet he surrendered to God's will. When a person is faced with the agonizing choice of continuing to obey God or quitting, yet they choose to carry on just like Jesus did. "Thy (Your refers to God) will be done." = A higher level surrendering and partnering with God Almighty. Matthew 26:42

God Given Destiny = Where one understands that they have been placed on this earth by Almighty God to fulfill a unique and special purpose that glorifies God and advances the Kingdom of God here on earth. Ephesians 2:10 NKJV "For we are His workmanship, created in Christ Jesus for good works, which God prepared beforehand that we should walk in them."

God Sized Calling = A mission/assignment from God that is impossible and overwhelming to accomplish in one's own strength. It is accomplished through a committed prayer life that brings forth strength, endurance, divine destiny helpers and resources to fulfill this destiny.

Godly Stewardship = Managing God's resources/blessings with skill, wisdom, and integrity.

Goliath(s) = Great adversaries who relentlessly oppress, torment, slander, harass the champions of justice through great wealth, power, influence, and varying means of manipulation. A symbolic reference of how David had to go against Goliath the giant who taunted and instilled fear in the Israelites. (1 Samuel 17)

Great Names of Justice/The Great Names/The Great = Humanitarians who partnered with God through a faithful prayer life to overcome intense opposition to achieve social justice even when it seemed impossible.

Greater Works = Disciples of Jesus Christ and/or The Great Names who achieve miraculous assignments, extraordinary accomplishments, those that are deemed impossible because of their prayer life and faith in Jesus Christ. John 14:12

Hardship = When one experiences misfortunes, tragedies, afflictions, sufferings but especially those that are extremely intense, hard to bear and harder to overcome.

Heaven = A beautiful place prepared for those who believe and have faith that Jesus Christ is the Son of God. A place where Father God, Jesus Christ and Angels reside and there is no more suffering, tears, pain, and death that is experienced here on earth.

"Hijacking of the Faith" = Using and manipulating the Christian Faith for one's own personal gain through unfair, racist, and immoral practices, laws, strategies, tactics, etc. through the false belief of the oppressed being inferior, and the oppressors are superior and "The Chosen people of God" (Revelations 2:9).

Humbleness/Humility = Understood that Jesus Christ of Nazareth must increase and become greater in their lives while they decrease and become less. John 3:30 Pointing others toward Jesus Christ and God Almighty not towards themselves. (Please note this humility is not "door mat theology".)

Injustice = Taken advantage of the poor and oppressing especially through "hijacking of the faith", religious manipulation; violations of their rights, a refusal to share wealth and other resources with the most vulnerable in society.

Justice = Ensuring the oppressed, the poor, the most vulnerable are protected, provided for, and released from oppression, hatred, racism, discrimination, poverty, and violence. It's distributive not just retributive.

Kingdom of God = A spiritual government that brings Heaven to earth through Jesus Christ and His sacrifice of laying down His life for the whole world to be saved. This type of government is not easily seen like worldly governments but those who are disciples of Jesus Christ of Nazareth and divine collaborators/ partners work to bring Heaven to earth through continual predestined good deeds (God Sized Calling, God Given Destiny)

Kuber-Ross Grief Cycle = The five stages of grief that one experiences after death, and other tragedies: divorce, termination/downsized, sick child, etc. The stages are Denial, Anger, Bargaining, Depression, & Acceptance. (Kubler-Ross, Elizabeth; On Death and Dying)

"Least of These"=Those who have been neglected, the most vulnerable, the poorest of the poor, the rejects and outcasts of society, those who are oppressed spiritually and naturally, (we have actually neglected Jesus). Symbolic Jesus in disguise. (Matthew 25:40-45)

Miracles, Signs & Wonders = Taken from the scriptures Matthew 10:8, Mark 16:17-18, John 14:12 that certain miracles, signs, wonders and greater works would follow Jesus Christ's (of Nazareth) disciples (healing, casting out demons, raising the dead), please note these are not the only signs. Great accomplishments that have been deemed impossible, prestigious awards, rewards and honors, large amounts of money donated/ fundraised on behalf of the God Calling.

Obedience = When one receives instructions from God Almighty one carries those instructions out with courage, determination, and humility.

Oppressor = Someone who uses spiritual manipulation, "hijacking of the faith" to steal and withhold resources from those who are deemed weaker, inferior, and villainized because of their race, ethnic identity, gender, religion, etc. and therefore deemed not intelligent enough to make serious choices about their wellbeing, rights, finances, education, healthcare, and housing.

Pass the Baton = A leader realizes the work they have given their life too; must continue after they are gone. Therefore, they train, prepare, and pray (successor prayer) for the next set of leaders to carry on with great success. They gladly pass the baton with grace, dignity, and love.

Peace = Where there is calm, order, stability, abundance; a true distributive and retributive justice.

Poverty = Where the least of these basic needs of food, finances, healthcare, housing, education are substandard or lacking all together that leads to violence because of systematic oppression, racism, and discrimination.

Prayer = A conversation, communication with God, where one talks to God and listens to God.

Prayer Empowerment Theory = The Great Names prayed first, and as God empowered them that prayer served as a solid foundation to JUSTICE, it catapulted them into strengthened and anointed action. It's comprised of four Core Outlines: Prayer Empowerment Theory, Prayer Foundation, Fight for Justice and Prayer Outcomes.

Prayer of Adoration (Adoration Prayer) = Where one worships and loves God in prayer, embodies loving God with your whole heart, mind, and soul.

Prayer of Empowerment (Empowered/Empowerment Prayer) = Being strengthened, anointed, and appointed by God Almighty for specific callings (tasks, assignments) that must be carried out with urgency, obedience, and determination.

Prayer of Forgiveness (Forgiveness Prayer) = Where one chooses to forgive their enemies, oppressors, goliaths, those who have harmed, oppressed, betrayed, and inflicted varying levels of damage to oneself, the least of these and others.

Prayer of Intercession (Intercessory Prayer) = Where one "stands in the gap" or gets in the spiritual battle of praying and sometime fasting to achieve a certain result or goal for someone else, a city, state, nation, etc. Especially those who can't pray or unable to get a prayer through to the Heavenly Father.

Prayer of Lament (Lamenting Prayer) = Where one pours out their heart of anguish, grief, disappointment and tears before God and asks for healing and strength to carry on, despite the hurts, setbacks, afflictions, and tragedies.

Prayer of Petitions/Requests (Petitioning Prayer) = Where one asks God sincerely for what he or she wants.

Prayer of Serenity (Serenity Prayer) = (Short Version) God grant me the Serenity to accept the things I cannot change, Courage to change the things I can, and Wisdom to know the difference.

Prayer of Silence(Silent Jesus Christ Centered Prayer) = Where one shows up, sits still in God's presence and is listening for God's voice. Embracing Psalm 46:10 Be still and know that I am God.

Prayer of Succession (Successor Prayer) = Where one prays for the success of the leader they will pass the baton too, a way to welcome the new leader(s) and ensure continuity of the GOD SIZED CALLING.

Prayer of Thanksgiving (Thanksgiving Prayer) = Where one tells God thank you for all He has done so far and thanks Him for all He is getting ready to do. (Thankful for the past, present and future help of God.)

Prayer Transformation = Where one grows through the stages of prayer until he or she is divine partner or collaborator with God. "Just don't ask what God can do for you, ask God what you can do for Him."

Religious Manipulators = A person who deliberately takes the Holy Bible out of context to oppress others by implying they are superior and the oppressed are inferior.

Righteous Indignation = An anger that comes from the injustices that are afflicted upon the "Least of These". An anger that says, "This must be stopped!"

Suffer = When one experiences intense losses and/or pain physically, emotionally, mentally, relationally, familially, financially, etc.

Surrender = When one yields to what God has instructed them to do (through prayer, dreams, visions, etc.), even when it is extremely difficult. Understanding God's perfected will supersedes the personal desires, thoughts, plans, and one's own will.

Tragedy = Intense suffering of the loss of relatives, friends, innocent children to murder or some other terrorist act, unable to see family, sickness, and disease. The heaviness of depression from things beyond one's control.

Villainized = A tactic used by Goliaths, Oppressors, Religious Manipulators to discredit, slander, assassinate The Great Names of Justice and the Least of These that they fight for by destroying their reputation, image, character through various forms of propaganda so they are not believed or trusted and to try and stop their fight for justice and to continue their oppression strategies.

Wilderness Preparation & Testing = Where God leads the person who said yes, into an intense season of equipping, training and building. God does this to test the person's heart to see if they will still obey Him in the toughest of circumstances and will they allow this season to humble them. The humility process is again a reminder that it is not about them, but about GOD and the person's dependency on GOD. Deuteronomy 8:2

Appendices F - Q

The Prayer Empowerment Theory Concept Maps

Appendix F – The Prayer Empowerment Theory Map

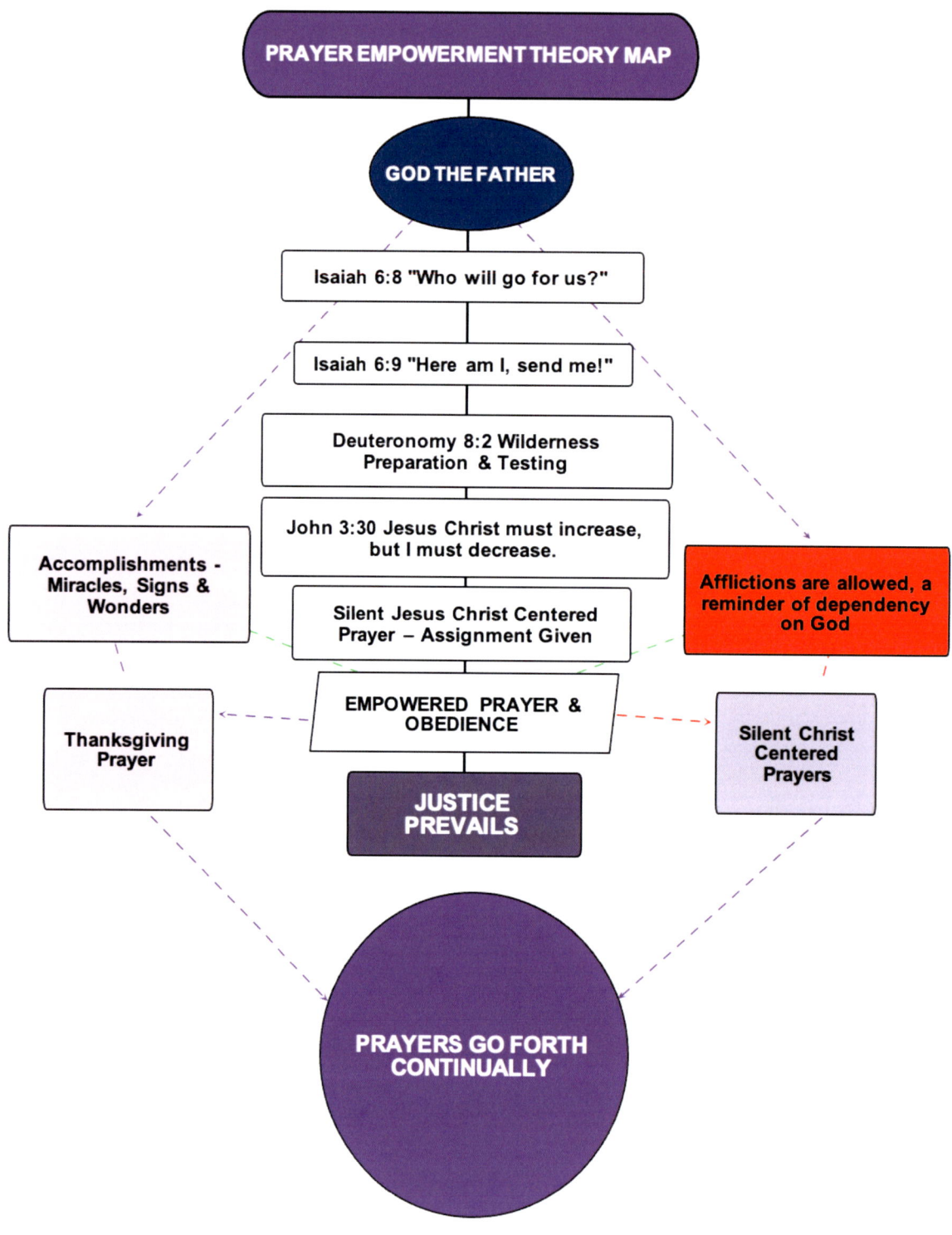

Appendix G – Prayer Transformation Map

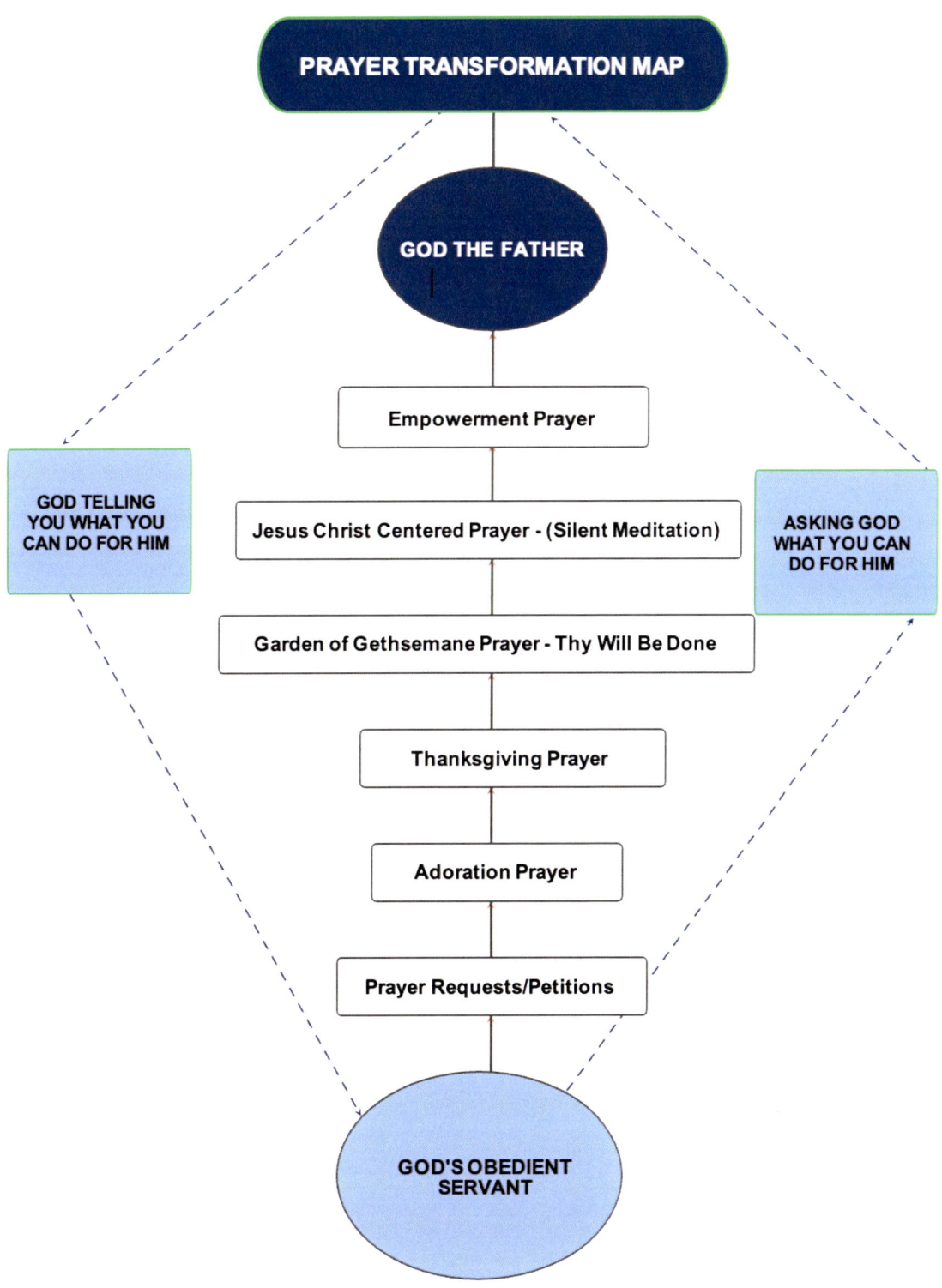

Appendix H – Acknowledges God Map

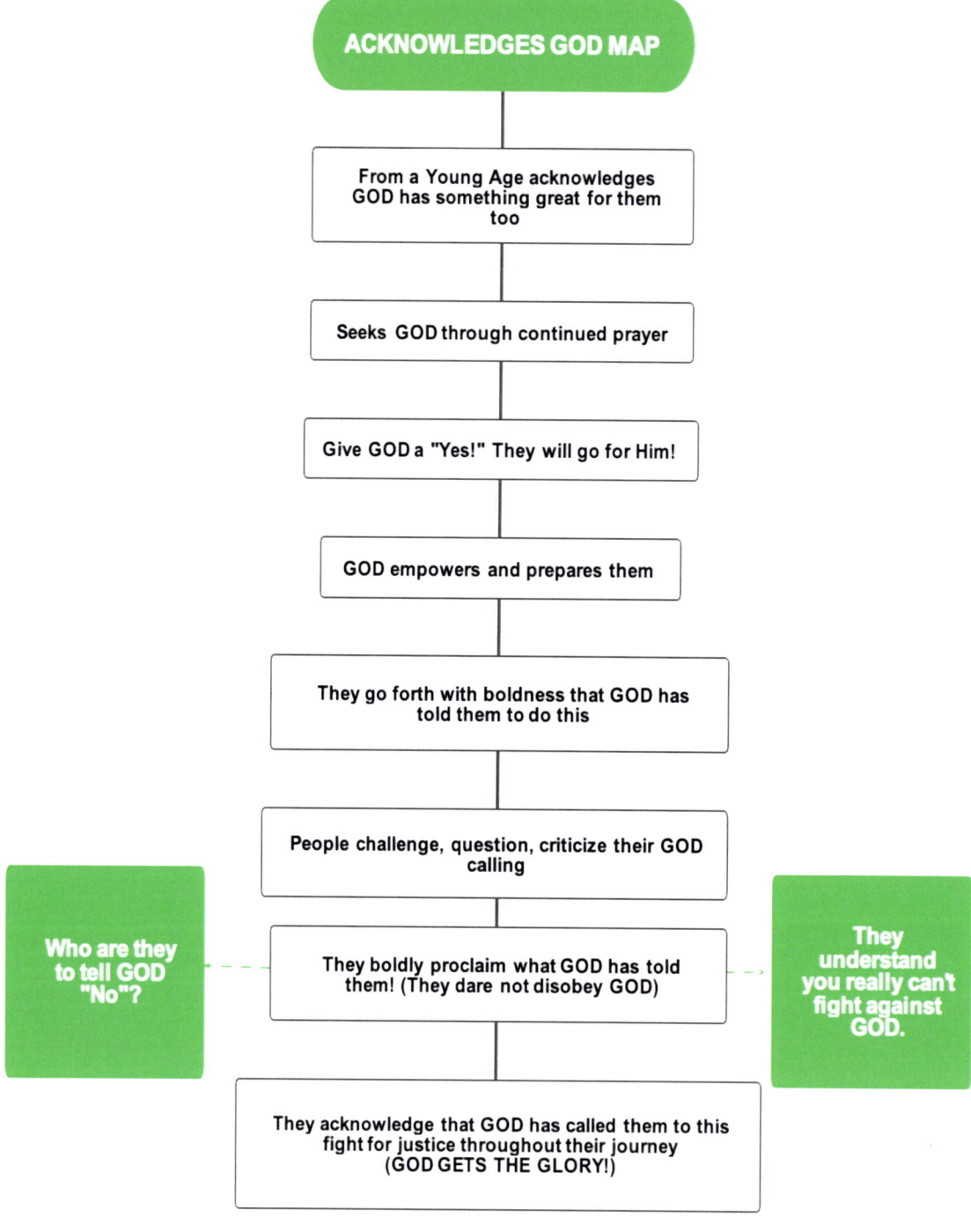

Appendix I – "Least of These" Map

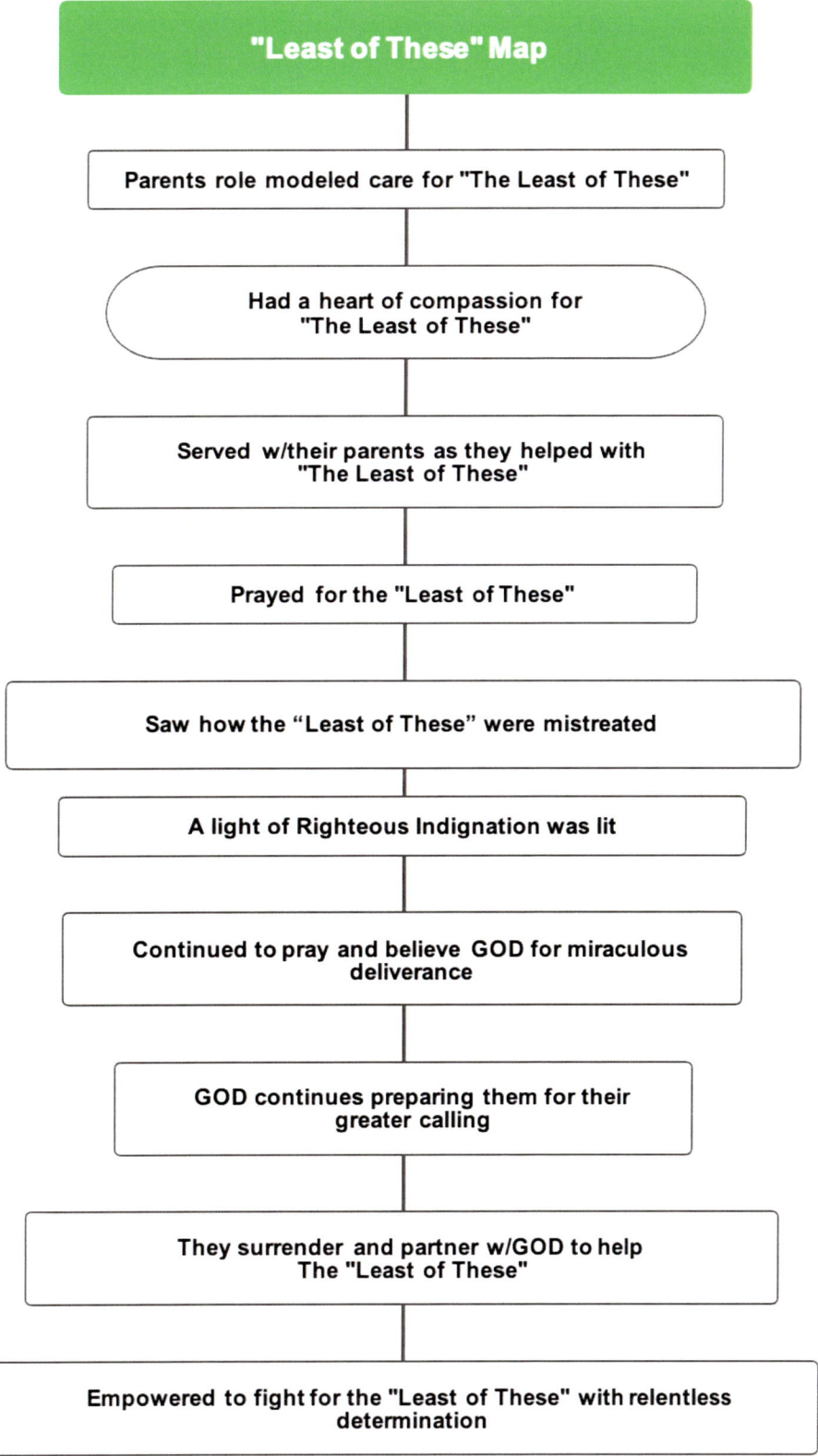

Appendix J – Identify Injustice Map

IDENTIFY INJUSTICE MAP

- Knew GOD created all people equal and should be treated as such
- Strong ability to identify injustice
- Knew hatred, poverty, oppression, racism were sins
- Rejected false Christianity that said one race was superior to all others
- Stood up against "hijacking of the (Christian) faith"
- Spoke out against all religious manipulators and their manipulations
- Stood on GOD's scriptures that He was the GOD of the oppressed, their DELIVERER!
- Prayed for strength, courage and endurance to keep fighting against injustice
- Empowered by God to set the captives free spiritually and naturally

Appendix K – Fighting Injustice Map

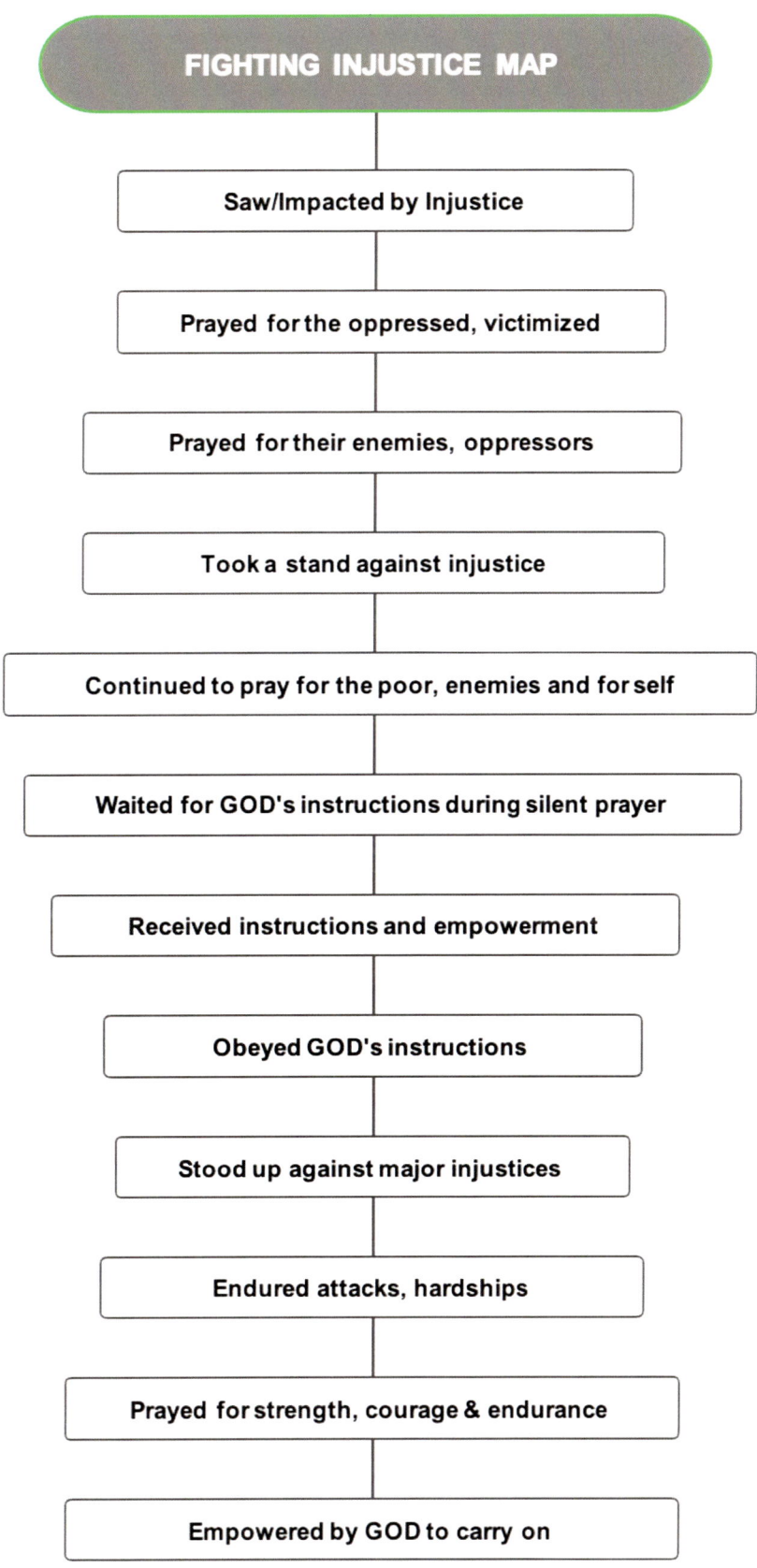

Appendix L – Dealing With Tragedy Map

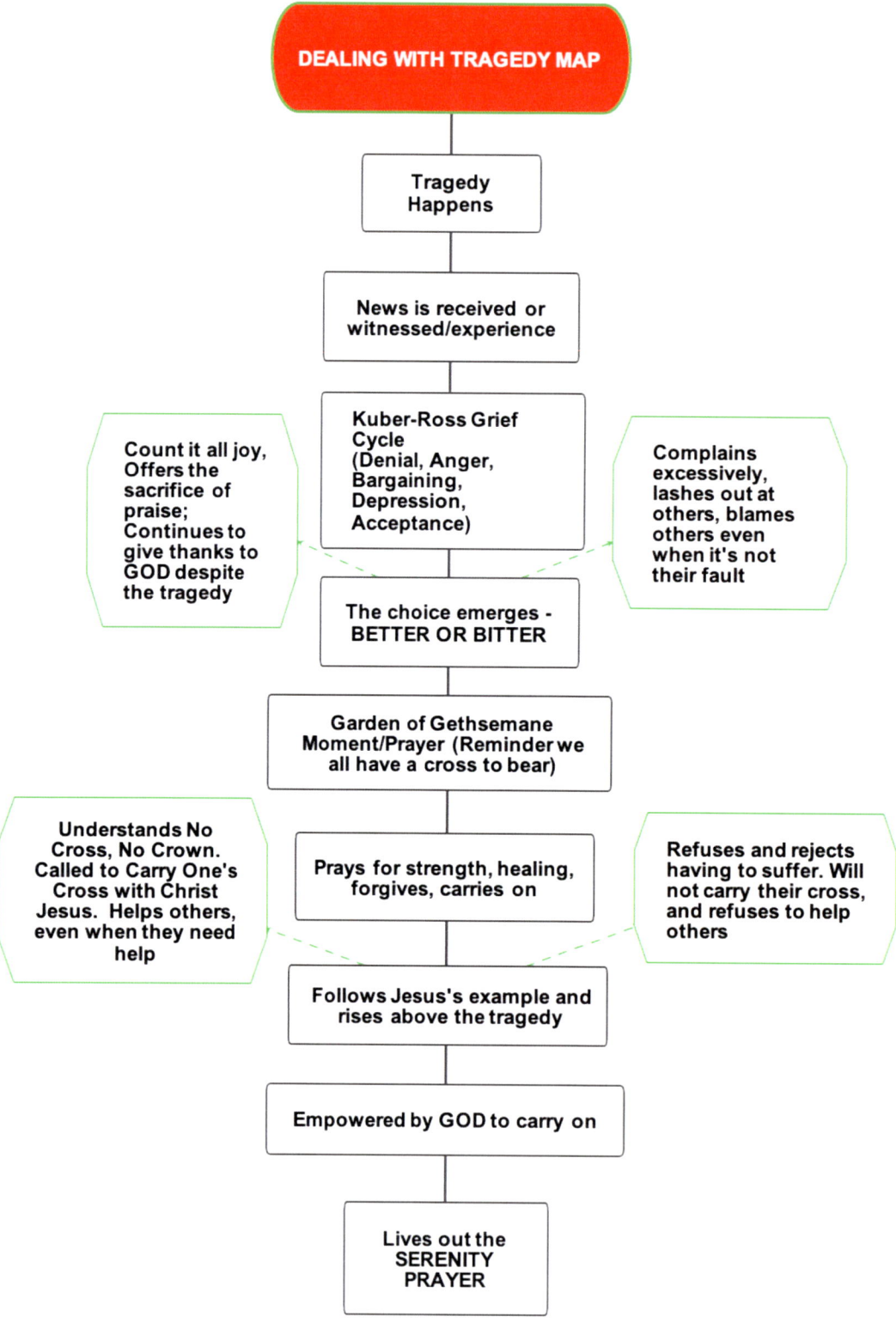

Appendix M – Obedience Map

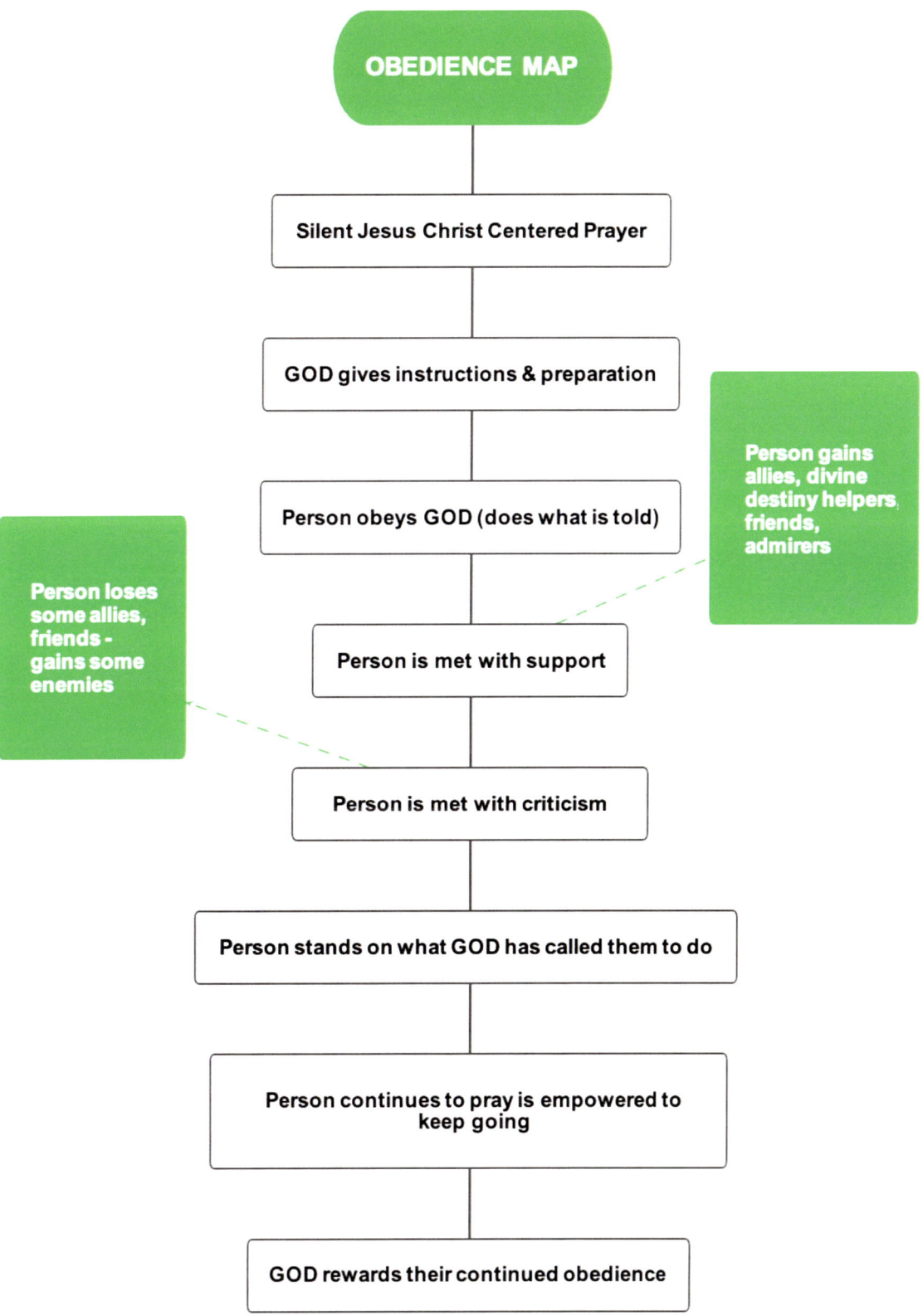

Appendix N – Miracles, Signs & Wonders Map

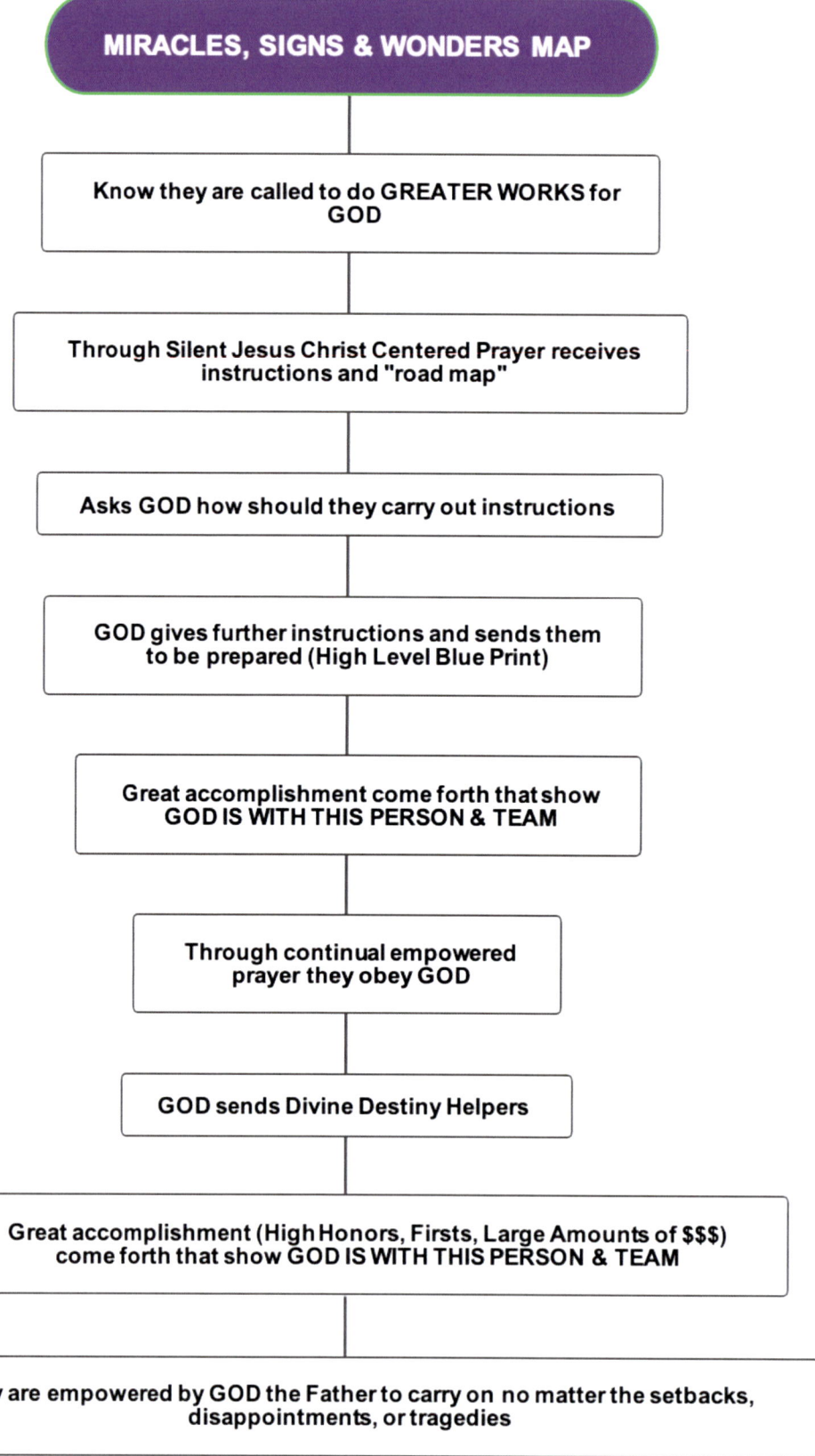

Appendix O – Pass the Baton Map

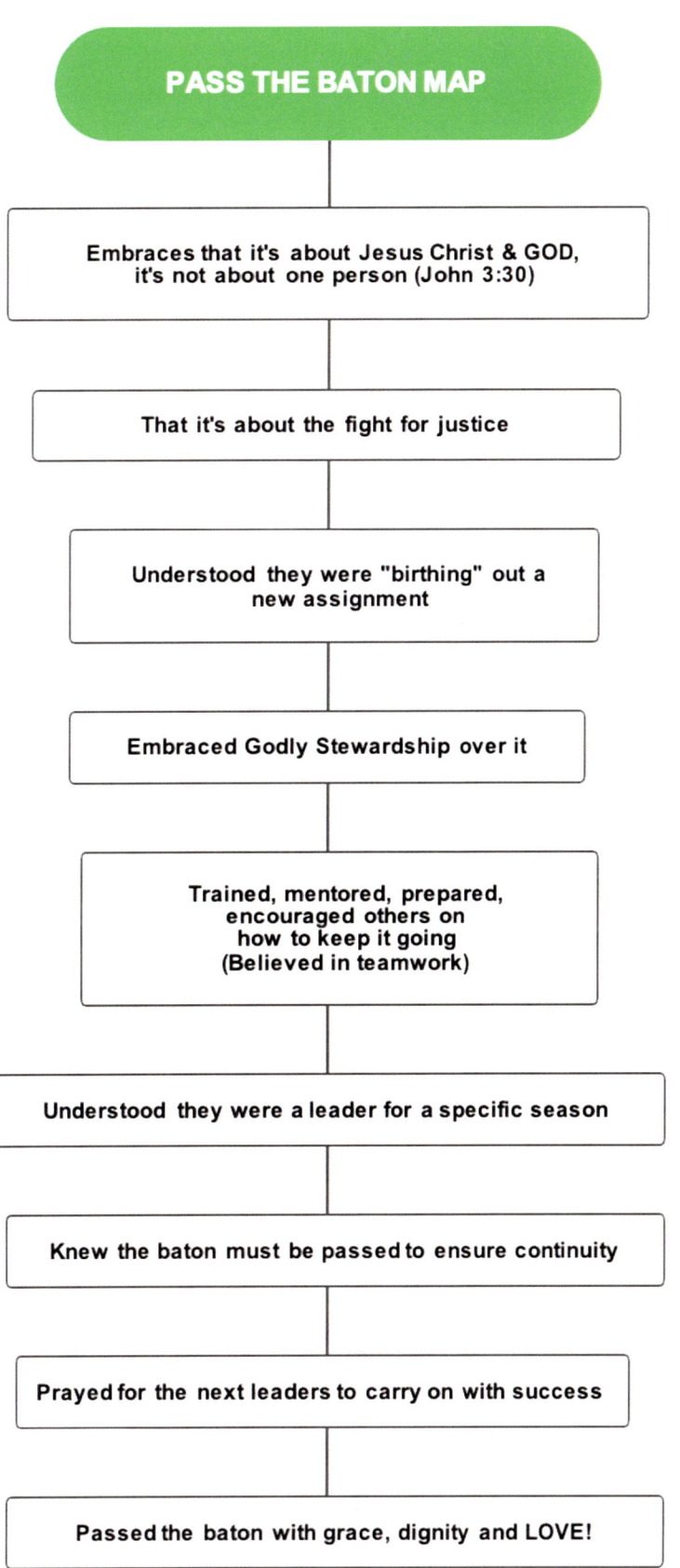

Appendix P – Great Follower to Great Leader Map

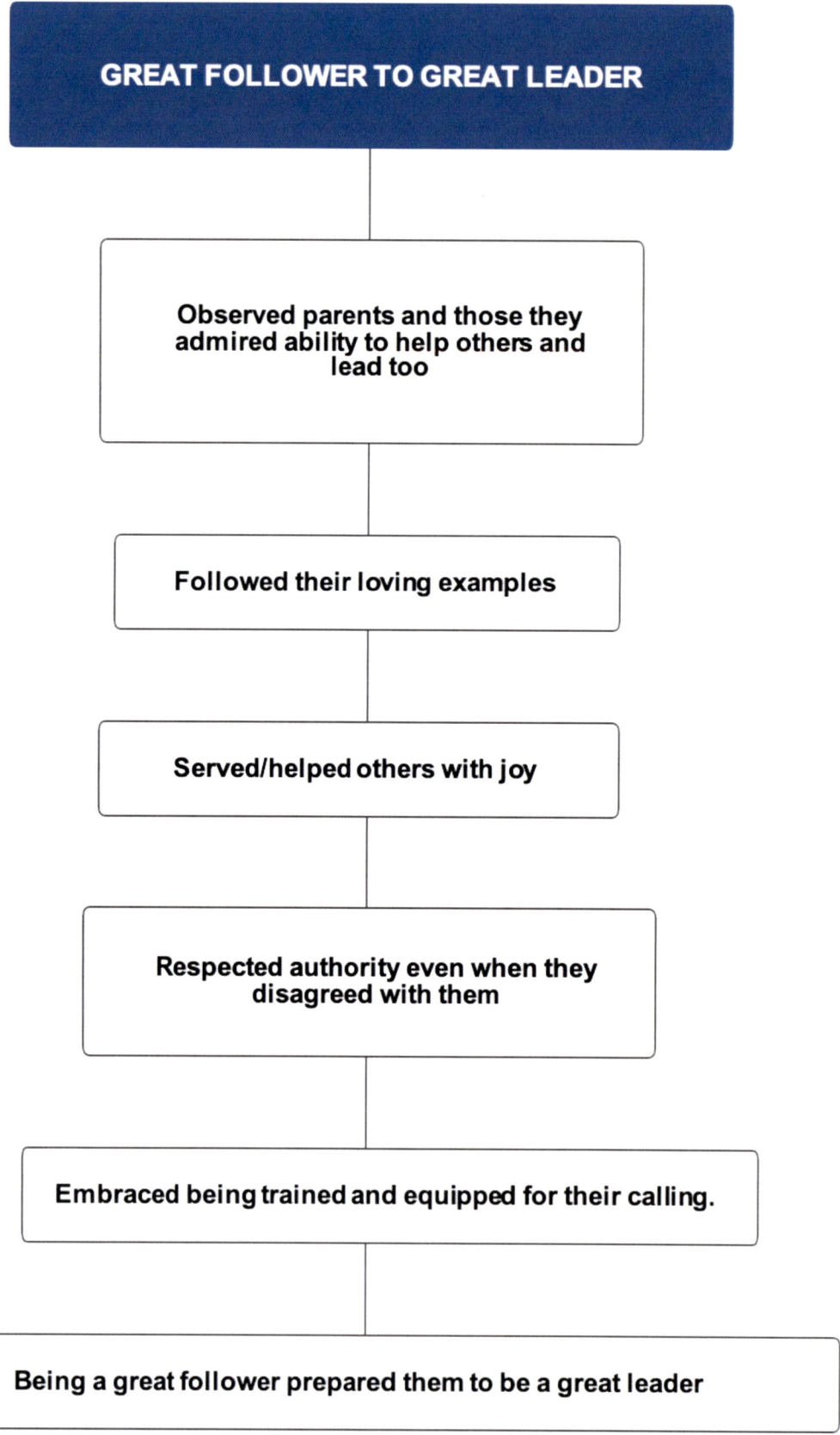

Appendix Q – Path to Greatness Map

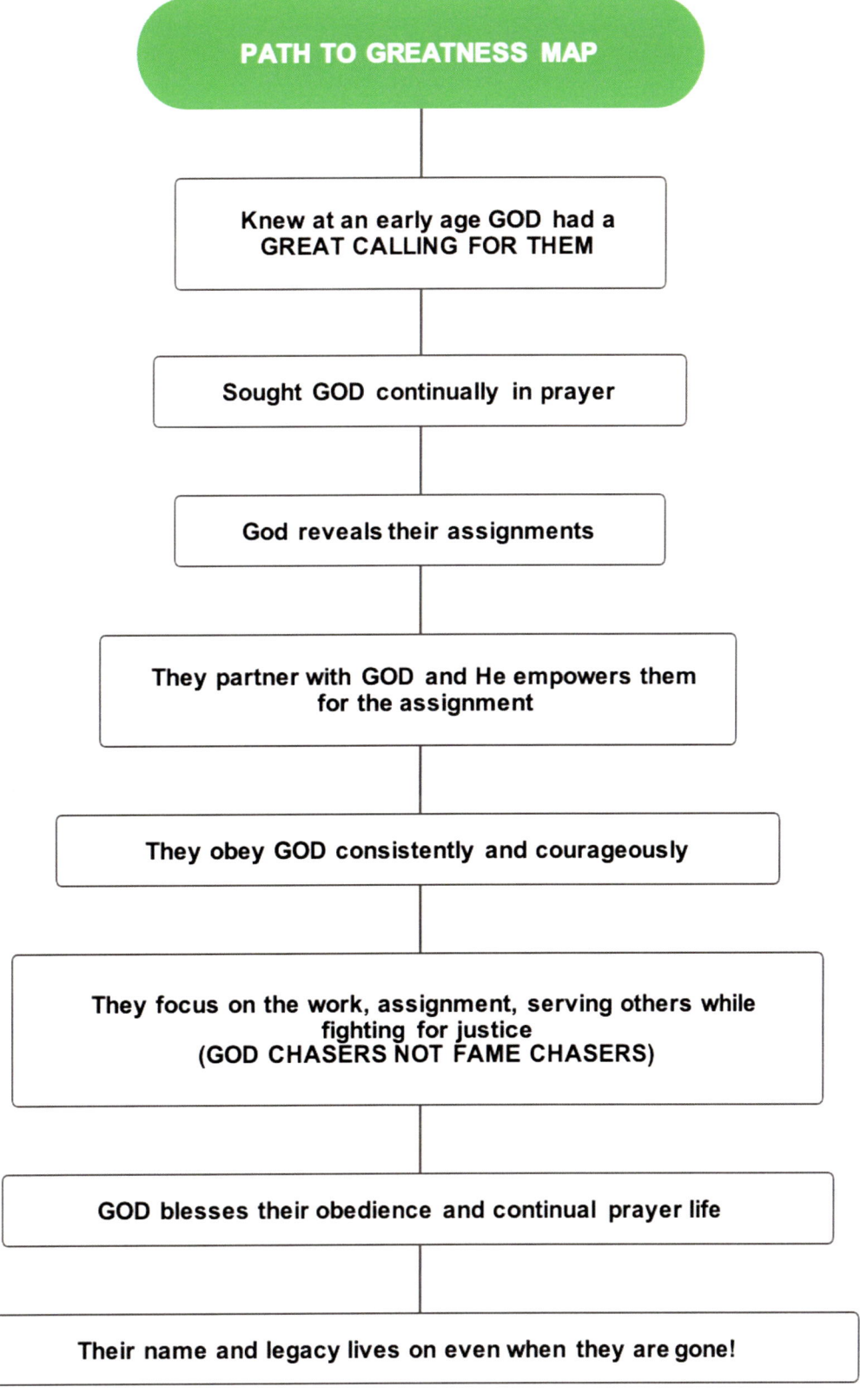

Appendix R - The Six Great Names Prayers

Appendix R – Six Great Names Prayers (1 of 2)

NELSON MANDELA (MANDIBA)	**Numbers 6:24-26 KJV** The LORD bless thee, and keep thee: The LORD make his face shine upon thee, and be gracious unto thee: The LORD lift up his countenance upon thee, and give thee peace.
	The Spiritual Mandela – Faith and Religion in the Life of Nelson Mandela by Dennis Cruywagen
RUBY BRIDGES-HALL	"Please, God, try to forgive those people. Because even if they say bad things. They don't know what they're doing. So, You could forgive them, Just like You did those folks a long time ago. When they said terrible things about You."
	The Story of Ruby Bridges by Robert Coles
DESMOND TUTU	"Thank you, God, for the spirit of unity and togetherness. Pour out your blessings on our leaders and their followers, to uphold the letter and spirit of this peace accord and beat our swords into plowshares. Send us forth to be instruments of your peace. Amen"
	Desmond Tutu: A Spiritual Biography of South Africa's Confessor by Michael Battle

Appendix R – Six Great Names Prayers (2 of 2)

CORETTA SCOTT KING	ETERNAL AND EVERLASTING GOD, WHO ART THE FATHER OF ALL MANKIND, AS WE TURN ASIDE FROM THE HURLY-BURLY OF EVERYDAY LIVING, MAY OUR HEARTS AND SOULS, YEA OUR VERY SPIRITS, BE LIFTED UPWARD TO THEE, FOR IT IS FROM THEE THAT ALL BLESSING COMETH. KEEP US EVER MINDFUL OF OUR DEPENDENCE UPON THEE, FOR WITHOUT THEE OUR EFFORTS ARE BUT NAUGHT. WE PRAY FOR THY DIVINE GUIDANCE AS WE TRAVEL THE HIGHWAYS OF LIFE. WE PRAY FOR MORE COURAGE. WE PRAY FOR MORE FAITH AND ABOVE ALL WE PRAY FOR MORE LOVE. MAY WE SOMEHOW COME TO UNDERSTAND THE TRUE MEANING OF THY LOVE AS REVEALED TO US IN THE LIFE, DEATH AND RESURRECTION OF THY SON AND OUR LORD AND MASTER, JESUS CHRIST. MAY THE CROSS EVER REMIND US OF THY GREAT LOVE, FOR GREATER LOVE NO MAN HATH GIVEN. THIS IS OUR SUPREME EXAMPLE, O GOD. MAY WE BE CONSTRAINED TO FOLLOW IN THE NAME AND SPIRIT OF JESUS, WE PRAY.
	"Prayers from African Americans in History" Prayers from African Americans in History - Beliefnet
MARTIN LUTHER KING JR	Eternal God out of whose mind this great cosmic universe we bless thee. Help us to seek that which is high, noble and Good. Help us in the moment of difficult decision. Help us to work with renewed vigor for a warless world, a better distribution of wealth, and a brotherhood that transcends race or color.
	("Thou, Dear God" Prayers That Open Hearts and Spirits - MLK Jr. by Lewis V. Baldwin)
MOTHER TERESA	Dear Jesus, help me to spread Thy fragrance everywhere I go. Flood my soul with Thy spirit and love. Penetrate and possess my whole being so utterly that all my life may only be a radiance of Thine. Shine through me and be so in me that every soul I come in contact with may feel Thy presence in my soul. Let them look up and see no longer me but only Jesus. Stay with me and then I shall begin to shine as you shine, so to shine as to be a light to others. Amen.
	"The Daily Prayer of Mother Teresa" The Daily Prayer of Mother Teresa (learnreligions.com)

Appendix S - Accomplishments vs. Afflictions

Appendix S - Accomplishments vs Afflictions (1 of 3)
MOTHER TERESA

(Highlights-Lists Are Not Complete)

ACCOMPLISHMENTS	**AFFLICTIONS**
1. Nobel Peace Prize	1. Never saw her mother and sister alive again, when she left as teenager.
2. Jawaharlal Nehru Award for International Understanding	2. Suffered at least two heart attacks
3. Bharat Ratna, the highest civilian honor in India	3. Hospitalized for pneumonia
4. Millions of Dollars in Donations for Missionary of Charities	4. Relentless verbal attacks by those who opposed her
5. Honor of Companion of the Order of Australia	5. Her life was in jeopardy on more than one occasion
6. Presidential Medal of Freedom	6. Had to view the casualties of war, violence and restlessness
7. Golden Honor of the Nation (Albania)	7. Denied the opportunity to see her mother and sister by the government
8. Missionary of Charities continues to grow and in several countries	8. Endured the stress of constant media attention

RUBY BRIDGES-HALL

(Highlights-Lists Are Not Complete)

ACCOMPLISHMENTS	**AFFLICTIONS**
1. Nobel Peace Prize (It's Coming)	1. Her life and family's lives were threatened
2. Honorary Deputy Marshall Award	2. Family suffered racism
3. Ruby Bridges Movie by Disney	3. She left behind a school, teachers and friends she really loved
4. Legacy of Caring Award	4. Endured isolation while integration William Jantz Elementary
5. Memoir "Through My Eyes"	
6. A Statue of Her at 6 years old is at William Jantz Elementary	
7. Integrated William Jantz Elementary	5. Lost her brother and son to senseless violence
8. Has shared her story with children and adults for over 25 years now	

Appendix S - Accomplishments vs Afflictions (2 of 3)
CORETTA SCOTT KING
(Highlights-Lists Are Not Complete)

ACCOMPLISHMENTS	AFFLICTIONS
1. Nobel Peace Prize (It's Coming)	1. Her husband MLK Jr. was assassinated
2. Devoted Wife of MLK Jr & Mother of 4 Beautiful Children	2. Had to carry on as Single Mother to four children
3. Implemented MLK Jr Day	3. Met with opposition of racism and sexism throughout her life
4. Raised Funds for the Civil Rights Movement	4. Endured home being bombed, death threats, etc.
5. Birthed out the MLK Jr Center, preserved MLK Jr and Kingian Legacy	5. When MLK Jr was locked/beat up, so was she symbolically
6. Raised Millions of Dollars for MLK Jr Center	6. Watched her husband and herself endure betrayals
7. Herself & MLK Jr Center trained South Africans for the 1st Democratic Election	7. Endured the painful tragedies of MLK Jr's mother, brother in a short 6 year time frame from MLK Jr's death
8. Civil Rights Activist & Global Social Justice Activist	8. Faced great opposition building the MLK Jr. Center

MARTIN LUTHER KING JR.
(Highlights-Lists Are Not Complete)

ACCOMPLISHMENTS	AFFLICTIONS
1. Nobel Peace Prize	1. Endured the bombing of their home, death threats, was stabbed
2. Youngest to receive Nobel Peace Prize	2. Arrested and detained illegally
3. Graduated early from High School & College, Married Coretta & Proud Dad to 4 Beautiful Children	3. Beaten unmercifully
	4. Did eulogies for children and fellow activists lost during the Civil Rights Movement
4. Leader of Civil Rights Movement	5. Accused of being a pacifist and communist
5. Known for his "I HAVE A DREAM SPEECH"	6. Had to travel extensively at times
	7. Reputation was slandered repeatedly
6. Inspired numerous individuals all over the world	8. He was assassinated
7. We live the "Dream" he saw	
8. Prayer-filled Leader whose legacy lives on	

Appendix S - Accomplishments vs Afflictions (3 of 3)
NELSON MANDELA
(Highlights – Lists Are Not Complete)

ACCOMPLISHMENTS	AFFLICTIONS
1. Nobel Peace Prize	1. Lost a nine month of baby girl to sickness suddenly (1ˢᵗ marriage)
2. 1ˢᵗ Elected Black South African President	2. Lost two marriages to the freedom movement
3. Demonstrated forgiveness & reconciliation at a very HIGH LEVEL	3. The Ravonia Trial could have ended in the "DEATH PENALTY" for him and comrades
4. Implemented the Truth & Reconciliation Commission	4. Spent 27 years of his "prime life" in Robben Island Prison
5. Achieved forgiveness, reconciliation and healing in South Africa	5. His mother, oldest son and several comrades died while in prison, was not allowed to attend their funerals
6. Known as "The Father of the Nation" & Mandiba	6. Limited amount of visitors and letters
7. Presidential Medal of Freedom Award & Numerous Prestigious Awards	7. Falsely accused of being a Communist, Atheist, & Terrorist
8. Ended the apartheid movement	

DESMOND TUTU
(Highlights – Lists Are Not Complete)

ACCOMPLISHMENTS	AFFLICTIONS
1. Nobel Peace Prize	1. Suffered respiratory infection at young age, impacted his health
2. Nominated/Elected Archbishop in South Africa unusually fast	2. Arrested/detained for fighting against apartheid
3. First black Appointed Anglican Dean of Johannesburg	3. Often misunderstood by colleagues, enemies, admirers, etc. in his prophetic calling by God
4. Numerous books have been written about him	4. Was beaten, suffered death threats
5. Appointed by President Mandela to lead the Truth & Reconciliation Commission	5. Traveled extensive with a very busy schedule
6. Presidential Medal of Freedom, Templeton Prize & numerous honors	6. Brought order to very challenging assignments
7. Anti-Apartheid Hero & Global Social Justice Activist	7. Falsely accused of being a Communist, Atheist & Terrorist

Bibliography

Allen, John *Rabble-Rouser For Peace – The Authorized Biography of Desmond Tutu* New York: Free Press, 2006

Baldwin, Lewis V. *"Thou, Dear God" – Prayers That Open Hearts and Spirits* Massachusetts: Beacon Press, 2012

Baldwin, Lewis V. *Never To Leave Us Alone – The Prayer Life of Martin Luther King Jr.* Minnesota: Fortress Press, 2010

Banks, Adelle M. 2017. "In her own words: Coretta Scott King on faith, materialism and grief." January 13th, 2017. https://religionnews.com/2017/01/13/in-her-own-wordscoretta-scott-king-on-faith-materialism-and-grief/

Battle, Michael *Desmond Tutu – A Spiritual Biography of South Africa's Confessor* Kentucky: Westminster John Knox Press, 2021

Beliefnet.com 2009. "Prayers from African Americans in History"https://www.beliefnet.com/faiths/prayer/2009/01/prayers-from-african-americans-inhistory.aspx

Beneate, Becky & Durepos, Joseph *Mother Teresa – No Greater Love* New York: MJF Boks, 1997

Bible Gateway, www.biblegateway.com. 1 Samuel 10:18, Deuteronomy 8:2, Exodus 5:1, Isaiah 6:8-9, Isaiah 58:12, Jeremiah 20:9, Psalm 76:9, Psalm 103:6, Psalm 146:7-8, Acts 10:38, John 3:30, John 4:34, John 5:30, John 6:38, Luke 23:34, Matthew 6:9-13, Matthew 25:31-46, Matthew 26:36-42, Mark 16:17-18, Numbers 6:24-26, 1 Corinthians 6:19-20, 1 Thessalonians 5:17, 2 Timothy 2:3-6 , and all other scriptures Accessed February – June 2023

Bolker, Joan *Writing Your Dissertation in Fifteen Minutes A Day – A Guide to Starting, Revising and Finishing Your Doctoral Thesis* New York: Holt Paperbacks, 1998

Bridges, Ruby *Ruby Bridges Goes to School :My True Story* New York: Scholastic Press, 2009

Bridges, Ruby *This Is Your Time* New York: Delacorte Press, 2020

Bridges, Ruby *Through My Eyes* New York: Scholastic Press, 1999

Campolo, Tony & Darling, Mary Albert *The GOD of Intimacy and Action – Reconnecting Ancient Spiritual Practices, Evangelism, and Justice* California: Jossey-Bass, 2007

City of Milwaukee. 2013. *Prayers for former President Nelson Mandela*. By Joe Davis, Sr. News Release https://city.milwaukee.gov/ImageLibrary/Groups/ccCouncil/2013-PDF/02--PrayersforMandela.pdf

City of Milwaukee. 2013. *Loss of Nelson Mandela felt in Milwaukee, worldwide*. By Joe Davis, Sr. News Release
https://city.milwaukee.gov/ImageLibrary/Groups/ccCouncil/2013-PDF/02-1205mandela.pdf

Clayton, Kimberly K. *It's Praying Time! – What You Need to Know About Prayer Intercession* Self Published, Written Words Publishing, 2021, 2022

Coles, Robert *The Story of Ruby Bridges* 25th ed., New York: Scholastic Press, 1995

Cooper, Brittney C. *Stand Up! : 10 Mighty Women Who Made a Change* New York: Orchard Books, 2022

Crosley, Jenna. 2021. "What (Exactly) Is Thematic Analysis? – Plain-Language Explanation & Definition (With Examples)" April 2021. https://gradcoach.com/what-is-thematicanalysis/

Crosley, Jenna. 2021. "What Is Qualitative Content Analysis? – QCA explained simply (with examples)" February 2021. https://gradcoach.com/qualitative-content-analysis/

Crossan, John Dominic *The Greatest Prayer – Rediscovering the Revolutionary Message of The Lord's Prayer* California: HarperOne, 2010

Cruywagen, Dennis *The Spiritual Mandela - Faith and Religion in the Life of Nelson Mandela* Massachusetts: Charlesbridge, 2018

Derosier, M. Michelle *Ruby Bridges : Get to Know the Girl. Who Took a Stand for Education* Minnesota: Capstone Press, 2019

Easton, Emily *ENOUGH! : 20 Protestors Who Changed America* Crown Books for Young Readers, 2018

"Everybody, Somebody, Anybody, Nobody Poem" Short Version Author Unknown

Faith Research. (date not listed) "Thinking of Jesus Motivates Us to Help Others But It May Depend on Your Faith" https://www.faithresearch.org/jesus-helping-motivation.html

Fincham, Frank (date not listed) "What Can Science Say About the Study of Prayer? – Separating Fact From Fiction in the Templeton Prayer Study" Florida State University. Accessed March 13th, 2023 https://www.templeton.org/news/what-can-science-sayabout-the-study-of-prayer

Gates Jr., Henry Louis *The Black Church (Entire Documentary)* Virginia: PBS Distribution, 2021

Goodreads.com; Quotes Churchill, Winston; Einstein, Albert; King Jr., Martin Luther and Unknown; retrieved December 2022

Gormley, Beatrice *Nelson Mandela : South African revolutionary*
New York: Aladdin, 2015

Grad Coach. 2021. "How To Write A Dissertation Or Thesis." Grad Coach Team. March 29th, 2021. Education video, https://youtu.be/1lr9z_O4P3A

Grant, Cynthia & Azadeh, Osanloo. 2014. "Understanding, Selecting and Integrating A Theoretical Framework in Dissertation Research: Creating the Blueprint for Your "House"."*Administrative Issues Journal* 4, no. 2 (2014): 12-26. https://eric.ed.gov/?id=EJ1058505 and https://files.eric.ed.gov/fulltext/EJ1058505.pdf

Gushee, David P. & Holtz, Colin *Moral Leadership For A Divided Age – Fourteen people who dared to change our world* Michigan: Brazos Press, 2018

Harrison, Vashti *Little Dreamers : Visionary Women Around the World* New York: Little, Brown and Company, 2018

Harrison, Vashti *Little Leaders : Bold Women in Black History* New York: Little, Brown and Company, 2017

"He who kneels before God, can stand before any man." Author Unknown

Hood, Susan *Shaking Things Up : 14 Young Women Who Changed the World* New York: Harpercollins Children's. Books, 2018

Hunt Ogden, Evelyn *Complete Your Dissertation or Thesis in Two Semesters or Less* Maryland: Roman & Littlefield Publishers, Inc., 2007

IJM/CRU Justice Studies III. 2023. "Justice and the Gospel". (blog) https://www.cru.org/us/en/train-and-grow/bible-studies/ijmcru-justice-studies-iii.html

Isbouts, Jean-Pierre *Ten Prayers That Changed the World* Washington DC: National Geographic Partners LLC, 2016

Jacobsen, Dennis A. *A Spirituality for Doing Justice : Reflections for Congregation-Based Organizer* Minnesota: Fortress Press, 2021

Jerome, Richard. "Mother Teresa – Her Life and Her Mission" Life, November 11th, 2022

Johnson, Melinda M. 2015. Building Bridges: Church Women United and Social Reform Work Across the Mid-Twentieth Century PhD diss., University of Kentucky.

Kelvie, Annie K. 2020. Rearticulating religious rhetoric: Literate activity and semiotic remediation in a progressive Christian church PhD diss., University of Illinois at Urbana Champaign https://www.ideals.illinois.edu/items/115726

Kibbe, Michael *From Topic To Thesis – A Guide To Theological Research* Illinois: InterVarsity Press, 2016

Knauer, Kelly *Nelson Mandela: A Hero's Journey TIME* New York: TIME BOOKS, 2013

Kolodiejchuk, Brian *Jesus is My All in All : Praying With "The Saint of Calcutta" Mother Teresa* New York: Doubleday, 2008

Kubler-Ross, Elisabeth *On Death and Dying (Kubler-Ross 5 Stages of Grief)* New York: Routledge, 1969

Ledford, David. 2021. "Prayer is Where the Action Is" *Absecon United Methodist Church* (blogpost) August 25h, 2021
https://abseconumc.com/blog/2021/08/25/prayer-is-wherethe-action-is

MacKinnon, Aran S. *Nelson Mandela : A Reference Guide to His Life and Works* Maryland: Rowman & Littlefield, 2020

Magoon, Kekla *Ruby Bridges – She Persisted* New York: Philomel Books, 2021

Makgoba, Thabo *Faith & Courage – Praying with Mandela* Ohio: Forward Movement, 2019

Mandela, Nelson, *Conversations With Myself* New York: Farrar Straus & Giroux, 2010

Mandela, Nelson *Long Walk to Freedom – The Autobiography of Nelson Mandela* New York: Back Bay Books/Little, Brown and Company: 1994

Mandela, Nelson *Nelson Mandela In His Own Words* New York: Back Bay Books/Little, Brown and Company, 2003

Mandela, Zindzi, Zazi, & Ziwelene *Grandad Mandela* Minnesota: Mandela Legacy, 2018

Missions Box. 2020. "Most Americans Pray But Disagree About How Prayer Works." (blogpost) 8/7/2020.
https://missionsbox.org/press-releases/most-americanspray-but-disagree-how-prayer-works/

Moore Jr., James P. *The Treasury of American Prayer* New York: Doubleday, 2008

Murray, Paul *I Loved Jesus in the Night – Teresa of Calcutta A Secret Revealed* Massachusetts: Paraclete Press, 2008

Natalie. 2022. "Conceptual and Theoretical Frameworks for Thesis Studies: What you must know". *Enago Thesis. Editing* (blogpost) June 2nd, 2022. https://www.enago.com/thesis-editing/blog/conceptual-and-theoretical-frameworks-forthesis-studies-what-you-must-know

Natalie. 2022. "Writing the Research Methodology Section of Your Thesis" *Enago Thesis Editing* (blogpost) September 2nd, 2022 https://www.enago.com/thesisediting/blog/writing-research-methodology-section-thesis

Nelson Mandela Exhibit – Prayer Journal of Nelson Mandela while in prison at Robben Island – Milwaukee Public Museum. July 16th, 2021 https://www.mpm.edu/MandelaEvents

Ogden, Charlie *Equality and Diversity* New York: Crabtree Publishing Company, 2017

Palcy, Euzhan, director. 1998. *Ruby Bridges*. Disney, DVD

Paradise, Brandon 2021 "Prayer and the Inner Life in the Struggle for Justice" Paper presented at 2021 Conference of the Institute for Eastern Christian Studies, Rutger Law School – Newark. https://papers.ssrn.com/sol3/papers.cfm?abstract_id=3988891

Pew Research Center. 2007 & 2014. "2014 Religious Landscape Study" Accessed March 14th, 2023 https://www.pewresearch.org/religion/religious-landscape-study/frequency-ofprayer/

Pew Research Center, Mohamed, Besheer; Cox, Kiana; Diamant, Jeff and Gecewicz, Claire. 2020. "Faith Among Black Americans – Religion & Politics" February 16th, 2021 https://www.pewresearch.org/religion/2021/02/16/religion-and-politics/

Pillay, Verashni. 2013. "Mandela and the confessions of a closet Christian" December 12th, 2013 https://mg.co.za/article/2013-12-12-mandela-and-the-confessions-of-acloset-christian/

Power, Samantha 2024 "The 100 Most Influential People of 2024" Times Magazine Accessed May 9th, 2024 https://time.com/6965206/diana-salazar/

Prayer and Action Coalition. 2020. "Biblical Principles for Just Policies in Policing and Criminal Justice" https://www.prayerandactioncoalition.org

Prayers & Action. 2023 "Joining Together to Become Part of the Solution to Gun Violence in this Country." https://prayersandaction.com/

Rackoczy, Susan 2023. "2023 Prayer or Action? The Tension Explored" *Finding Solace* (blogpost) https://www.findingsolace.org/prayer-or-action-the-tension-explored/

Riead, William, director. 2016 *The Letters*. Twentieth Century Fox Home Entertainment, DVD

Rogers, Kristen. 2020. "The Psychological benefits of prayer: What Science says about the mind-soul connection." CNN Health Accessed March 14th, 2023 https://www.cnn.com/2020/06/17/health/benefits-of-prayer-wellness/index.html

Ruby Bridges Exhibit, *"The Problem We All Still Live With"* in   *The Power of Children: Making a Difference* at The Children's Museum Indianapolis November 25th, 2016 & May 9th, 2024 https://www.childrensmuseum.org/blog/ruby-bridges-and-problem-we-all-still-live

Schwarz, Tanya B. *Faith-Based Organizations in. Transnational Peacebuilding* London: Roman & Littlefield International, Ltd, 2018

Scott King, Coretta & Reynolds, Barbara *My Life, My Love, My Legacy* New York: Henry Holt and Company, 2017

Sebba, Anne *Mother Teresa – Beyond the Image* New York: Doubleday, 1997

"Serenity Prayer" Author Unknown 1933

Sohail, K. *Prophets of Violence, Prophets of Peace* Green Zone Publishing, 2013

Spector, Nicole. 2017 Rev. 2018. "This is Your Brain on Prayer and Meditation" BETTER Today NBC News, Accessed March 13th, 2023 https://www.nbcnews.com/better/health/your-brain-prayer-meditation-ncna812376

Stalnacke, Mari-Anna. 2021. "Prayer Requires Action" *Flowing Faith* (blogpost) January 19th, 2021 https://flowingfaith.com/2021/01/prayer-requires-action.html

Sullivan, Anne Marie *Mother Theresa* Pennsylvania: Mason Crest, 2003

Thoughtco. 2018. "The Daily Prayer of Mother Teresa" *Learn Religions* (blogpost) Updated August 28th, 2018. https:// https://www.learnreligions.com/daily-prayer-of-mother-teresa542274

Tiffin University, Pfeifer Library. 2022. "What Are Research Methods"
August 2nd, 2022
https://library.tiffin.edu/researchmethodologies/whatareresearchmethods#s-lg-box25345878

Turabian, Kate L. *A Manual for Writers of Research, Papers, Theses, and Dissertations* 9th ed. Illinois: The University of Chicago Press, 2018

Tutu, Desmond *God's Dream* Massachusetts: Candlewick Press, 2008

Tutu, Naomi *The Words of Desmond Tutu* New York: Newmarket Press, 1989

Valdesolo, Piercarlo. 2013. "Scientists Find One Source of Prayer's Power – Communing with a higher power increases self-control". Scientific American. Accessed. March 13th, 2023
https://www.scientificamerican.com/article/scientists-find-one-source-of-prayerspower/

Zammataro, Jeanne & United Church of Christ Economic Justice League. 2015. *A Six Week Study Guide for The Greatest Prayer* New York, Harpers Collins Publisher https://new.uccfiles.com/pdf/Greatest-Prayer.pdf

About the Author

&

My Prayer For You

About the Author

Dr. Kimberly K. Clayton earned her Master's in Biblical Studies, Christian Counseling Certificate, and Community Chaplain credential from Ecclesia Leadership Institute (2017-2019). She is an author of several books all available on itsprayingtime.net (2021-2022, 2024):

1. It's Praying Time – What You Need To Know About Prayer Intercession
2. It's Praying Time & Soul Winning Time
3. It's Praying Time & Humility Is Required
4. It's Praying Time & No More Idols
5. It's Praying Time & Obedience Is Required
6. Called to Intercede Vol. 1 (Co-Author) – Ch.44 "Jesus Prayed and Still Does"
7. An Intercessor's Pain
8. PRAYER THE FOUNDATION FOR JUSTICE

Kimberly K. Clayton successfully started and published her Doctor of Ministry from 2020-2024 from Ecclesia Leadership Institute.

Prayer has made such a difference in Kimberly's life and it's her desire that more people come to know that the power of prayer works, they accept Jesus Christ and live for Him too.

She is also the founder of It's Praying Time and Women Destined For Greater on YouTube (youtube.com/@ItsPrayingTime & youtube.com/@womendestinedforgreater). You can also check out www.itsprayingtime.com and www.womendestinedforgreater.com.

If you haven't accepted Jesus Christ as the Son of God and Lord & Savior please say this
Salvation Prayer:

Dear Lord Jesus, I know that I am a sinner, and I ask you for your forgiveness. I believe you died for my sins and rose from the dead. I turn from my sins, and invite You to come into my heart and life. I ask for the Holy Spirit to dwell in me, to guide me, and to teach me all things. I choose to trust and follow You as the Son of God and LORD and Savior in Jesus name Amen and Amen.

Your next steps are:

• Download the Bible App and read the Bible every day.
https://www.youversion.com/the-bible-app/

• Also get a good paper Parallel Study Bible with KJV and NLT, or NKJV and your choice of translation.

• Pray that God will lead you to a good church home where you can be planted, rooted, and established in the Word of God.

MY PRAYER FOR YOU

Heavenly Father I pray that the person reading this book will draw closer to you and ask what can be done for you? When the answer is given the person is empowered to carry out the assignment with love, humility, courage, faithfulness, joy and determination until it is finished. That you will encourage this person to keep going and to never give up in Jesus Mighty Name Amen.

www.ingramcontent.com/pod-product-compliance
Lightning Source LLC
Chambersburg PA
CBRC101143030426
42337CB00008B/63